Summary

Congress has debated the efficacy and constitutionality of federal regulation of firearms and ammunition, with strong advocates arguing for and against greater gun control. Since March 2011, much of the gun control debate in the 112th Congress has swirled around allegations that the Department of Justice (DOJ) and the Bureau of Alcohol, Tobacco, Firearms and Explosives (ATF) mishandled a Phoenix, AZ-based gun trafficking investigation known as "Operation Fast and Furious." In the Consolidated and Further Continuing Appropriations Act, 2012 (P.L. 112-55), Congress included a provision that reflects a Senate-adopted amendment that forbids the expenditure of any funding provided under it to be used by a federal law enforcement officer to transfer an operable firearm to a person known or suspected to be connected with a drug cartel without that firearm being continuously monitored or controlled. The act, however, does not include language adopted during House full committee markup to prohibit ATF from collecting multiple long gun sales reports in Southwest border states. Meanwhile, Congress continues to consider the implications of Operation Fast and Furious and several gun control issues.

On May 10, 2012, the House passed a measure (H.R. 5326) that would fund ATF for FY2013. On April 19, 2012, the Senate Committee on Appropriations also reported a bill (S. 2323) that would fund ATF for FY2013. Both bills include several gun control-related provisions. On April 17, 2012, the House passed the Sportsmen's Heritage Act of 2012 (H.R. 4089), a bill that would prohibit any federal agency from banning recreational shooting on federally managed public lands. On November 16, 2011, the House passed a bill (H.R. 822) that would establish a greater degree of reciprocity between states that issue concealed carry permits for handguns to civilians than currently exists under state law. On October 11, 2011, the House passed a Veterans' Benefits Act (H.R. 2349) that would prohibit the Department of Veterans Affairs from determining a beneficiary to be mentally incompetent for the purposes of gun control, unless such a determination were made by a judge, magistrate, or other judicial authority based upon a finding that the beneficiary posed a danger to himself or others. In May 2011, firearms-related amendments to bills reauthorizing the USA PATRIOT Act were considered (H.R. 1800, S. 1038, and S. 990), but they were not passed.

The tragic shootings in Tucson, AZ, on January 8, 2011, in which 6 people were killed and 13 wounded, including Representative Gabrielle Giffords, have also generated attention. Several Members introduced proposals that arguably address issues related to the shooter's mental illness and drug use (see S. 436/H.R. 1781) and his use of large capacity ammunition feeding devices (LCAFDs) (see H.R. 308 and S. 32), as well as a proposal to ban firearms within the proximity of certain high-level federal officials (see H.R. 367 and H.R. 496).

This report concludes with discussion of other salient and recurring gun control issues that have generated past congressional interest. Those issues include (1) screening firearms background check applicants against terrorist watch lists, (2) reforming the regulation of federally licensed gun dealers, (3) requiring background checks for private firearms transfers at gun shows, (4) more-strictly regulating certain firearms previously defined in statute as "semiautomatic assault weapons," and (5) banning or requiring the registration of certain long-range .50 caliber rifles, which are commonly referred to as "sniper" rifles. To set these and other emerging issues in context, this report provides basic firearms-related statistics, an overview of federal firearms law, and a summary of legislative action in the 111th and 112th Congresses.

Contents

Figures

Tables

Appendixes

Contacts

Developments in the 112th Congress

Since March 2011, much of the gun control debate in the 112th Congress has swirled around allegations that the Department of Justice (DOJ) and the Bureau of Alcohol, Tobacco, Firearms and Explosives (ATF) mishandled a Phoenix, AZ-based gun trafficking investigation known as "Operation Fast and Furious." In December 2010, two suspect firearms, and possibly a third, linked to that investigation were found at the murder scene of Border Patrol Agent Brian Terry. In January 2010, ATF whistleblowers contacted Senator Charles Grassley with assertions that suspected gun traffickers had not been arrested in a timely fashion and, and as a result, a large number of suspect firearms had not been interdicted and have reportedly passed into the hands of drug traffickers and other criminals. The whistleblowers referred to this investigative tactic as "gun walking." According to one source, 665 of these firearms have been recovered by law enforcement at crime scenes on both sides of the border.[1] Another 1,355 suspect firearms reportedly remain unaccounted for.

Senator Grassley, ranking minority Member on the Committee on the Judiciary, and Representative Darrell Issa, chairman of the Committee on Oversight and Government Reform, have issued two joint staff reports on Operation Fast and Furious, and the House committee has held four related hearings, the most recent on February 2, 2012. Representative Elijah Cummings, the committee's ranking minority Member, has also issued two reports related to this controversial operation. On November 1, 2011, a high-ranking DOJ official testified before the Senate Committee on the Judiciary's Crime and Terrorism Subcommittee that he had identified "gun walking" as a potentially risk laden investigative technique in April 2010 but failed to inform the Attorney General about the potential risks. On November 8, 2011, the Senate Committee on the Judiciary held a DOJ oversight hearing, and Attorney General Eric Holder fielded questions about Operation Fast and Furious. The Attorney General conceded that a February 4, 2011, letter from DOJ to congressional investigators contained "inaccurate" information regarding the depth of knowledge that departmental officials had of ATF's use of the "gun walking" tactic. On December 8, 2011, the House Committee held a hearing to explore, among other things, whether senior departmental officials knew more about Operation Fast and Furious than what was previously indicated in a May 3, 2011, hearing before that committee.

On November 18, 2011, the President signed into law the Consolidated and Further Continuing Appropriations Act, 2012 (H.R. 2112; P.L. 112-55), following House and Senate passage on the previous day. This act provides ATF with $1.152 billion for FY2012. In response to Operation Fast and Furious, Congress included in that act a provision (§219) that reflects a Senate-passed amendment sponsored by Senator John Cornyn to prevent the expenditure of any funding provided under it to be used by a federal law enforcement officer to facilitate the transfer of an operable firearm to a person known to be or suspected of being connected to a drug cartel without that firearm being continuously monitored or controlled. The act, however, does not include an amendment that was sponsored by Representative Denny Rehberg and adopted in House full committee markup that would have prevented ATF from collecting multiple long gun sales reports from federally licensed gun dealers in Southwest border states. In addition, two ATF funding provisos and one Federal Bureau of Investigation (FBI) funding proviso were made

---

[1] Pete Yost, "Fast and Furious-Like 'Gun-Walking' Probe Mentioned In 2007 Bush Administration Memo," *Huffington Post,* November 4, 2011.

permanent, as opposed to annual appropriations restrictions. These provisos essentially prohibit the consolidation or centralization of firearm acquisition and disposition records.

In its FY2013 DOJ budget submission, the Administration proposed dropping the Cornyn language related to "gun walking," arguing that the prohibition is unnecessary. The Administration also proposed stripping the futurity language out of the ATF and FBI funding provisions. In addition, the Administration proposed stripping futurity language out of a long-standing but controversial provision known as the Tiahrt amendment, which prohibits ATF from releasing firearms trace data under a range of circumstances. Besides including futurity language, Congress has altered the language of the Tiahrt amendment several times in recent years to clarify under which circumstances and at what level of detail it is proper to release firearms trace data to law enforcement and other governmental officials, as well as to researchers, the media, and the general public.

Other legislative developments in the 112th Congress include the following:

- On May 10, 2012, the House passed a measure (H.R. 5326) that would fund ATF for FY2013 at $1.151 billion. This measure includes the Cornyn anti-gun walking provision, and would make several additional ATF appropriations riders permanent law by including futurity language in those provisions, instead of following the Administration's proposal and stripping futurity language out of the provisions that were made permanent law in the FY2012 appropriations cycle. The House-passed bill also includes a provision that would prohibit ATF from collecting long gun sales reports. This provision reflects a Rehberg amendment that was successfully offered in full committee markup.

- On May 3, 2012, Representative Darrell Issa, Chairman of the House Oversight and Government Reform Committee, issued a staff briefing paper to committee Members that included a draft resolution to cite the Attorney General with contempt for not fully complying with committee subpoenas for information about Operation Fast and Furious and other matters.

- On April 19, 2012, the Senate Committee on Appropriations reported a bill (S. 2323) that would fund ATF for FY2013 at $1.153 billion. This bill includes the Cornyn provision, but it does not include anything similar to the Rehberg amendment. Like the House bill, it does not address the Administration's proposal to strip futurity language out of the provisions that were made permanent law in the FY2012 appropriations cycle, but it would not make any additional provisos permanent law.

- On April 17, 2012, the House passed the Sportsmen's Heritage Act of 2012 (H.R. 4089), a bill that would prohibit any federal agency from banning recreational shooting on federally managed public lands.

- On November 16, 2011, the House passed a bill (H.R. 822) that would establish a greater degree of reciprocity between states that issue concealed carry permits for handguns to civilians than currently exists under state law. The Senate considered a similar amendment, which was narrowly defeated, in the 111th Congress.

- On October 11, 2011, the House passed a Veterans' Benefits Act (H.R. 2349). This bill includes a provision that would prohibit the Department of Veterans Affairs from determining a beneficiary to be mentally incompetent for the purposes of gun control, unless such a determination were made by a judge, magistrate, or other judicial authority based upon a finding that the beneficiary posed a danger to himself or others. Similar proposals were considered in either the House or the Senate in the 110th and 111th Congresses, in the wake of the enactment of the NICS Improvement Amendments Act of 2007 (P.L. 110-180).[2]

- During May 2011, firearms-related amendments were offered to bills to extend certain USA PATRIOT Act provisions related to national security investigations (H.R. 1800, S. 1038, and S. 990), but those amendments were not passed.

The 112th Congress could also examine issues potentially arising from the tragic shootings in Tucson, AZ, on January 8, 2011, in which 6 people were killed and 13 wounded, including Representative Gabrielle Giffords. Armed with a 9mm Glock 19 semiautomatic pistol loaded with a 33-round extended magazine, the shooter reportedly fired 31 shots before bystanders were able to subdue him while he was attempting to reload with another 33-round extended magazine. He also carried two additional 15-round magazines.[3] As discussed below, these magazines were previously defined under federal law as large capacity ammunition feeding devices (LCAFDs) and were banned for 10 years, from September 13, 1994, through September 13, 2004, as part of the larger semiautomatic assault weapons ban. Legislation has been introduced to reinstate the LCAFD ban (H.R. 308 and S. 32) and to ban firearms within the proximity of certain high-level federal officials (H.R. 367 and H.R. 496). Congressional interest could also focus on the shooter's mental illness and illegal drug use.

- On November 15, 2011, the Senate Committee on the Judiciary's Subcommittee on Crime and Terrorism held a hearing on the Fix Gun Checks Act of 2011 (S. 436/H.R. 1781). This proposal would amend P.L. 110-180 to advance certain deadlines and apply deeper cuts to a wider array of federal law enforcement assistance grant programs to incentivize the greater sharing of firearms-related disqualifying records. Congress passed P.L. 110-180 in the wake of the tragic April 16, 2007, Virginia Tech shootings.

Background and Analysis

Pro/Con Debate

Through the years, legislative proposals to restrict the availability of firearms to the public have raised the following questions: What restrictions on firearms are permissible under the Constitution? Does gun control constitute crime control? Can the nation's rates of homicide, robbery, and assault be reduced by the stricter regulation of firearms commerce or ownership? Would restrictions stop attacks on public figures or thwart deranged persons and terrorists? Would household, street corner, and schoolyard disputes be less lethal if firearms were more difficult and expensive to acquire? Would more restrictive gun control policies have the unintended effect of impairing citizens' means of self-defense?

---

[2] NICS stands for the National Instant Criminal Background Checks System, which is described below.

[3] David von Drehle, "1 Madman and a Gun: 15 Seconds to Fire the Glock; 31 Bullets in One Clip; 19 Victims, with Six Killed," *Time*, January 24, 2011, p. 26.

In recent years, proponents of gun control legislation have often held that only *federal* laws can be effective in the United States. Otherwise, they say, states with few restrictions will continue to be sources of guns that flow illegally into more-restrictive states. They believe that the Second Amendment to the Constitution, which states that "[a] well regulated Militia, being necessary to the security of a free State, the right of the people to keep and bear Arms shall not be infringed," is being misread in today's modern society. They argue that the Second Amendment (1) is now obsolete, with the presence of professional police forces; (2) was intended solely to guard against suppression of state militias by the central government and is therefore restricted in scope by that intent; and (3) does not guarantee a right that is absolute, but rather one that can be limited by reasonable requirements. They ask why in today's modern society a private citizen needs any firearm that is not designed primarily for hunting or other recognized sporting purposes.

Proponents of firearms restrictions have advocated policy changes on specific types of firearms or components that they believe are useful primarily for criminal purposes or that pose unusual risks to the public. Fully automatic firearms (i.e., machine guns) and short-barreled rifles and shotguns have been subject to strict regulation since 1934. Fully automatic firearms have been banned from private possession since 1986, except for those legally owned and registered with the Secretary of the Treasury as of May 19, 1986. More recently, "Saturday night specials" (loosely defined as inexpensive, small handguns), "assault weapons," ammunition-feeding devices with capacities for more than seven rounds, and certain ammunition have been the focus of control efforts.

Opponents of gun control vary in their positions with respect to specific forms of control but generally hold that gun control laws do not accomplish what is intended. They argue that it is as difficult to keep weapons from being acquired by "high-risk" individuals, even under federal laws and enforcement, as it was to stop the sale and use of liquor during Prohibition. In their view, a more-stringent federal firearms regulatory system would only create problems for law-abiding citizens, bring mounting frustration and escalation of bans by gun regulators, and possibly threaten citizens' civil rights or safety. Some argue that the low violent crime rates of other countries have nothing to do with gun control, maintaining instead that multiple cultural differences are responsible.

Gun control opponents also reject the assumption that the only legitimate purpose of ownership by a private citizen is recreational (i.e., hunting and target-shooting). They insist on the continuing need of people for effective means to defend themselves and their property, and they point to studies that they believe show that gun possession lowers the incidence of crime. They say that the law enforcement and criminal justice system in the United States has not demonstrated the ability to furnish an adequate measure of public safety in all settings. Some opponents further believe that the Second Amendment includes a right to keep arms as a defense against potential government tyranny, pointing to examples in other countries of the use of firearms restrictions to curb dissent and secure illegitimate government power. The debate has been intense.

To gun control advocates, the opposition is out of touch with the times, misinterprets the Second Amendment, and is lacking in concern for the problems of crime and violence. To gun control opponents, advocates are naive in their faith in the power of regulation to solve social problems, bent on disarming the American citizen for ideological or social reasons, and moved by irrational hostility toward firearms and gun enthusiasts.

Gun-Related Statistics

Crime and mortality statistics are often used in the gun control debate. According to a recent study, however, none of the existing sources of statistics provide either comprehensive, timely, or accurate data with which to definitively assess whether there is a causal connection between firearms and violence.[4] For example, existing data do not show whether the number of people shot and killed with semiautomatic assault weapons declined during the 10-year period (1994-2004) that those firearms were banned from further proliferation in the United States.[5] Presented below are data on the following topics: (1) the number of guns in the United States, (2) firearms-related homicides, (3) non-lethal firearms-related victimizations, (4) gun-related mortality rates, (5) use of firearms for personal defense, and (6) recreational use of firearms. In some cases, the data presented are more than a decade old but remain the most recent available.

How Many Guns Are in the United States?

The National Institute of Justice (NIJ) reported in a national survey that in 1994, 44 million people, approximately 35% of households, owned 192 million firearms, 65 million of which were handguns.[6] Seventy-four percent of those individuals were reported to own more than one firearm.[7] According to the ATF, by the end of 1996 approximately 242 million firearms were available for sale to or were possessed by civilians in the United States.[8] That total includes roughly 72 million handguns (mostly pistols, revolvers, and derringers), 76 million rifles, and 64 million shotguns.[9] By 2000, the number of firearms had increased to approximately 259 million: 92 million handguns, 92 million rifles, and 75 million shotguns.[10] By 2007, the number of firearms had increased to approximately 294 million: 106 million handguns, 105 million rifles, and 83 million shotguns.[11]

In the past, most guns available for sale were produced domestically. In recent years, 1 million to 2 million handguns were manufactured each year, along with 1 million to 1.5 million rifles and fewer than 1 million shotguns.[12] From 2001 through 2007, however, handgun imports nearly doubled, from 711,000 to nearly 1.4 million.[13] By 2009, nearly 2.2 million handguns were imported into the United States.[14] From 2001 through 2007, rifle imports increased from 228,000

---

[4] National Research Council, *Firearms and Violence: A Critical Review* (Washington, DC: 2005), p. 48.

[5] Ibid., p. 49.

[6] Jens Ludwig and Phillip J. Cook, *Guns in America: National Survey on Private Ownership and Use of Firearms*, NCJ 165476, May 1999, http://www.ncjrs.org/pdffiles/165476.pdf.

[7] Ibid.

[8] U.S. Department of the Treasury, Bureau of Alcohol, Tobacco and Firearms, *Commerce in Firearms in the United States*, February 2000, pp. A3-A5.

[9] Ibid., pp. A3-A5.

[10] U.S. Department of the Treasury, Bureau of Alcohol, Tobacco and Firearms, *Firearms Commerce in the United States 2001/2002*, ATF P 9000.4, April 2002, pp. E1-E3.

[11] U.S. Department of Justice, Bureau of Alcohol, Tobacco, Firearms and Explosives (ATF), *Annual Firearm Manufacturing and Export Reports for 2002 through 2007*, along with firearms import data provided by the ATF Firearms and Explosives Import Branch.

[12] Ibid.

[13] U.S. Department of Justice, Bureau of Alcohol, Tobacco, Firearms and Explosives, Firearms and Explosives Import Branch.

[14] U.S. Department of Justice, Bureau of Alcohol, Tobacco, Firearms and Explosives, *Firearms Commerce in the* (continued...)

---

to 632,000, and shotgun imports increased from 428,000 to 726,000.[15] By 2009, rifle imports had increased to 864,000, but shotguns had decreased 559,000.[16] By the same year, 2009, the estimated total number of firearms available to civilians in the United States had increased to approximately 310 million: 114 million handguns, 110 million rifles, and 86 million shotguns.[17]

Retail prices of guns vary widely, from $75 or less for inexpensive, low-caliber handguns to more than $1,500 for higher-end, standard-production rifles and shotguns.[18] Data are not available on the number of "assault weapons" in private possession or available for sale, but one study estimated that 1.5 million assault weapons were privately owned in 1994.[19]

How Often Are Guns Used in Homicides?

As **Table 1** shows, reports submitted by state and local law enforcement agencies to the FBI and published annually in the *Uniform Crime Reports*[20] indicate that the firearms-related murder and non-negligent manslaughter rate per 100,000 of the population decreased from 6.6 for 1993 to 3.6 for 2000. The rate held steady at 3.6 for 2001 and fluctuated thereafter between a high of 3.9 for 2006 and 2007, and a low of 3.2 for 2010.

Table 1. Firearms-Related Murder and Non-negligent Manslaughter Victims, 1993-2010

Year	Murder Victims	Rate per 100,000 of the Population	Estimated Firearms-Related Murder and Non-negligent Manslaughter Victims[a]	Rate per 100,000 of the Population
1993	24,526	9.5	17,073	6.6
1994	23,326	9.0	16,333	6.3
1995	21,606	8.2	14,727	5.6
1996	19,645	7.4	13,261	5.0
1997	18,208	6.8	12,335	4.6
1998	16,974	6.3	11,006	4.1
1999	15,522	5.7	10,117	3.7
2000	15,586	5.5	10,203	3.6

(...continued)

United States 2011, August 2011, p. 15.

[15] U.S. Department of Justice, Bureau of Alcohol, Tobacco, Firearms and Explosives, Firearms and Explosives Import Branch.

[16] U.S. Department of Justice, Bureau of Alcohol, Tobacco, Firearms and Explosives, *Firearms Commerce in the United States 2011*, August 2011, p. 15

[17] Ibid., pp. 11, 13, and 15.

[18] Ned Schwing, *2005 Standard Catalog of Firearms: The Collector's Price and Reference Guide*, 15th edition (Iola, Wisconsin, 2005).

[19] Christopher S. Koper, *Updated Assessment of the Federal Assault Weapons Ban: Impacts on Gun Markets and Gun Violence, 1994-2003* (Washington, DC: July 2004).

[20] See http://www.fbi.gov/ucr/ucr.htm.

Year	Murder Victims	Rate per 100,000 of the Population	Estimated Firearms-Related Murder and Non-negligent Manslaughter Victims[a]	Rate per 100,000 of the Population
2001	16,037	5.6	10,139	3.6
2002	16,229	5.6	10,841	3.8
2003	16,528	5.7	11,037	3.8
2004	16,148	5.5	10,665	3.6
2005	16,740	5.6	11,363	3.8
2006	17,309	5.8	11,731	3.9
2007	17,128	5.7	11,631	3.9
2008	16,645	5.4	11,029	3.6
2009	15,399	5.0	10,301	3.4
2010	14,748	4.8	9,958	3.2

Source: CRS compilation of FBI crime statistics reported annually in the *Uniform Crime Reports*, 1993-2010.

a. The number of firearms-related murder and non-negligent manslaughter victims was estimated by applying the percentage of firearms-related murders for which the cause of death was known to the number of all reported murder and non-negligent homicide victims for which the cause was known or unknown.

How Prevalent Are Gun-Related Fatalities?

The source of national data on firearms deaths is the publication *Vital Statistics*, published each year by the National Center for Health Statistics. Firearms deaths reported by coroners are presented in five categories: homicides, legal interventions,[21] suicides, accidents, and unknown circumstances. For these categories, the data are presented below for 1993 through 2007 in two tables, one for all deaths and the other for juvenile deaths.

Table 2. Firearms-Related Deaths for All Ages

1993-2009

Year[a]	Homicides	Legal Interventions	Suicides	Accidents	Unknown	Total Deaths	% Change
1993	18,253	318	18,940	1,521	563	39,596	
1994	17,527	339	18,765	1,356	518	38,506	-2.8%
1995	15,551	284	18,503	1,225	394	35,958	-6.6%
1996	14,037	290	18,166	1,134	413	34,041	-5.3%
1997	13,252	270	17,566	981	367	32,437	-4.7%
1998	11,798	304	17,424	866	316	30,709	-5.3%
1999	10,828	299	16,599	824	324	28,875	-6.0%
2000	10,801	270	16,586	776	230	28,664	-0.7%

[21] "Legal interventions" include deaths (in these cases by firearms) that involve legal uses of force (justifiable homicide or manslaughter), usually by the police.

Year[a]	Homicides	Legal Interventions	Suicides	Accidents	Unknown	Total Deaths	% Change
2001	11,348	323	16,869	802	231	29,574	3.2%
2002	11,829	300	17,108	762	243	30,243	2.3%
2003	11,920	347	16,907	730	232	30,137	-0.4%
2004	11,624	311	16,750	649	235	29,570	-1.9%
2005	12,352	330	17,002	789	221	30,695	3.8%
2006	12,791	360	16,883	642	220	30,897	0.7%
2007	12,632	351	17,352	613	276	31,224	1.1%
2008	12,179	326	18,223	592	273	31,593	1.1%
2009	11,493	333	18,735	554	232	31,347	-0.7

Source: National Center for Health Statistics.

a. As of February 28, 2012, the last year for which data were available was calendar year 2009.

As **Table 2** shows, firearms fatalities decreased continuously from 39,595 in 1993 to 28,664 in 2000, for an overall decrease of nearly 28%. Compared with firearms deaths in 2000, such deaths increased by 3.2% in 2001 to 29,574, and increased again, by 2.3%, in 2002 to 30,243. They decreased by 0.3% in 2003 to 30,137, and decreased again, by 1.9%, in 2004 to 29,570. Firearms fatalities increased by 3.8% in 2005 to 30,694, by 0.7% in 2006 to 30,897, and by 1.1% in 2007 to 31,224. They increased again by 1.1% in 2008, but decreased by 0.7% in 2009. Of the 2009 total, 11,826 were homicides or due to legal intervention, 18,735 were suicides, 554 were unintentional (accidental) shootings, and 232 were of unknown causes.[22]

As **Table 3** shows, there were 1,520 juvenile (younger than 18 years old) firearms-related deaths in 2007. Of the juvenile total, 1,047 were homicides or due to legal intervention, 325 were suicides, 112 were unintentional, and 36 were of unknown causes. From 1993 to 2001, juvenile firearms-related deaths decreased by an average rate of 10% annually, for an overall decrease of 56%. From 2001 to 2002, such deaths increased slightly (by less than 1%), but declined by nearly 9% from 2002 to 2003. They increased from 2002 through 2006, by 5% to 7%, but decreased by nearly 5% in 2007.[23] Juvenile firearms-related fatalities decreased again by 3.0% in FY2008 and nearly 6% in 2009.

Table 3. Firearms-Related Deaths for Juveniles

1993-2009

Year[a]	Homicides	Legal Interventions	Suicides	Accidents	Unknown	Total Deaths	% Change
1993	1,975	16	832	392	76	3,292	
1994	1,912	20	902	403	81	3,319	0.8%
1995	1,780	16	836	330	72	3,035	-8.6%

---

[22] National Vital Statistics System data taken from the Injury Statistics Query and Reporting System (WISQARS), http://www.cdc.gov/ncipc/wisqars/default.htm.

[23] Ibid.

Year[a]	Homicides	Legal Interventions	Suicides	Accidents	Unknown	Total Deaths	% Change
1996	1,473	9	720	272	49	2,524	-16.8%
1997	1,308	7	679	247	43	2,285	-9.5%
1998	1,045	17	648	207	54	1,972	-13.7%
1999	1,001	9	558	158	50	1,777	-9.9%
2000	819	15	537	150	23	1,545	-13.1%
2001	835	6	451	125	16	1,434	-7.2%
2002	872	7	423	115	26	1,444	0.7%
2003	805	8	377	102	25	1,318	-8.7%
2004	868	6	384	105	22	1,386	5.2%
2005	921	5	412	127	25	1,491	7.6%
2006	1,082	14	371	102	24	1,594	6.9%
2007	1,038	9	325	112	36	1,520	-4.6%
2008	984	6	361	98	26	1,475	-3.0%
2009	887	5	401	83	16	1,392	-5.6%

Source: National Center for Health Statistics.

a. As of February 28, 2012, the last year for which data were available was calendar year 2009.

How Often Are Guns Used in Non-lethal Crimes?

The other principal source of national crime data is the *National Crime Victimization Survey* (NCVS) conducted by the U.S. Census Bureau and published by the Bureau of Justice Statistics (BJS). The NCVS database provides some information on the weapons used by offenders, based on victims' reports. Based on data provided by survey respondents in calendar year 2009, BJS estimated that, nationwide, there were 4.3 million non-lethal violent crimes (rape or sexual assault, robbery, aggravated assault, and simple assault).[24] Weapons were used in 22% of these incidents, and firearms were used by offenders in 8% of these incidents.[25] The estimated number of firearms-related non-lethal violent crime incidents decreased from 428,670 in 2000 to 326,090 in 2009, and from 2.4 persons to 1.4 per 100,000 of the population ages 12 and older.[26]

How Often Are Firearms Used in Self-Defense?

According to BJS, NCVS data from 1987 to 1992 indicate that in each of those years, roughly 62,200 victims of violent crime (1% of all victims of such crimes) used guns to defend themselves.[27] Another 20,000 persons each year used guns to protect property. Persons in the

---

[24] U.S. Department of Justice, Bureau of Justice Statistics, National Crime Victimization Survey, *Criminal Victimization, 2009*, by Jennifer L. Truman and Michael R. Rand, p. 8.

[25] Ibid.

[26] Ibid.

[27] U.S. Department of Justice, Office of Justice Programs, Bureau of Justice Statistics, *Guns and Crime: Handgun Victimization, Firearm Self-Defense, and Firearm Theft*, NCJ-147003, April 1994, http://bjs.ojp.usdoj.gov/content/pub/ (continued...)

---

business of self-protection (police officers, armed security guards) may have been included in the survey.[28] Another source of information on the use of firearms for self-defense is the National Self-Defense Survey conducted by criminology professor Gary Kleck of Florida State University in the spring of 1993. Citing responses from 4,978 households, Dr. Kleck estimated that handguns had been used 2.1 million times per year for self-defense, and that all types of guns had been used approximately 2.5 million times a year for that purpose during the 1988-1993 period.[29]

Why do these numbers vary by such a wide margin? Law enforcement agencies do not collect information on the number of times civilians use firearms to defend themselves or their property against attack. Such data have been collected in household surveys. The contradictory nature of the available statistics may be partially explained by methodological factors. That is, these and other criminal justice statistics reflect what is *reported* to have occurred, not necessarily the actual number of times certain events occur. Victims and offenders are sometimes reluctant to be candid with researchers. So, the number of incidents can only be estimated, making it difficult to state with certainty the accuracy of statistics such as the number of times firearms are used in self-defense. For this and other reasons, criminal justice statistics often vary when different methodologies are applied.

Survey research can be limited because it is difficult to produce statistically significant findings from small incident populations. For example, the sample in the National Self-Defense Survey might have been too small, given the likely low incidence rate and the inherent limitations of survey research.

What About the Recreational Use of Guns?

According to NIJ, in 1994 recreation was the most common motivation for owning a firearm.[30] There were approximately 15 million hunters, about 35% of gun owners, in the United States, and about the same number and percentage of gun owners engaged in sport shooting in 1994.[31] The U.S. Fish and Wildlife Service (FWS) reported that there were more than 14.7 million persons who were paid license holders in 2003[32] and, according to the National Shooting Sports Foundation, in that year approximately 15.2 million persons hunted with a firearm and nearly 19.8 million participated in target shooting.[33] The FWS reported that there were 14.4 million paid license holders in 2010.[34]

(...continued)

ascii/hvfsdaft.txt.

[28] Ibid.

[29] Gary Kleck, "Armed Resistance to Crime: The Prevalence and Nature of Self-Defense with a Gun," *Journal of Criminal Law and Criminology*, vol. 86, issue 1, 1995, http://www.guncite.com/gcdgklec html.

[30] Jens Ludwig and Phillip J. Cook, *Guns in America: National Survey on Private Ownership and Use of Firearms*, NCJ 165476, May 1999, p. 2.

[31] Ibid., p. 3.

[32] U.S. Department of the Interior, U.S. Fish and Wildlife Service, *National Hunting License Report* (December 2, 2004).

[33] American Sports Data, Inc., *The SUPERSTUDY of Sports Participation*.

[34] U.S. Department of the Interior, U.S. Fish and Wildlife Service, *National Hunting License Report* (December 10, 2010).

Federal Regulation of Firearms

Two major federal statutes regulate the commerce in and possession of firearms: the National Firearms Act of 1934 (26 U.S.C. §5801 et seq.) and the Gun Control Act of 1968, as amended (18 U.S.C. Chapter 44, §921 et seq.). Supplementing federal law, many state firearms laws are stricter than federal law. For example, some states require permits to obtain firearms and impose a waiting period for firearms transfers. Other states are less restrictive, but state law cannot preempt federal law. Federal law serves as the minimum standard in the United States.

The National Firearms Act (NFA)

The NFA was originally designed to make it difficult to obtain types of firearms perceived to be especially lethal or to be the chosen weapons of "gangsters," most notably machine guns and short-barreled long guns. This law also regulates firearms, other than pistols and revolvers, which can be concealed on a person (e.g., pen, cane, and belt buckle guns). It taxes all aspects of the manufacture and distribution of such weapons, and it compels the disclosure (through registration with the Attorney General) of the production and distribution system from manufacturer to buyer.

The Gun Control Act of 1968 (GCA)

As stated in the GCA, the purpose of federal firearms regulation is to assist federal, state, and local law enforcement in the ongoing effort to reduce crime and violence. In the same act, however, Congress also stated that the intent of the law is not to place any undue or unnecessary burdens on law-abiding citizens in regard to the lawful acquisition, possession, or use of firearms for hunting, trapshooting, target shooting, personal protection, or any other lawful activity.

The GCA, as amended, contains the principal federal restrictions on domestic commerce in small arms and ammunition. The statute requires all persons manufacturing, importing, or selling firearms *as a business* to be federally licensed; prohibits the interstate mail-order sale of all firearms; prohibits interstate sale of handguns generally and sets forth categories of persons to whom firearms or ammunition may not be sold, such as persons under a specified age or with criminal records; authorizes the Attorney General to prohibit the importation of non-sporting firearms; requires that dealers maintain records of all commercial gun sales; and establishes special penalties for the use of a firearm in the perpetration of a federal drug trafficking offense or crime of violence.

As amended by the Brady Handgun Violence Prevention Act, 1993 (P.L. 103-159), the GCA requires background checks be completed for all non-licensed persons seeking to obtain firearms from federal firearms licensees. Private transactions between persons "not engaged in the business" are not covered by the recordkeeping or the background check provisions of the GCA. These transactions and other matters such as possession, registration, and the issuance of licenses to firearms owners may be covered by state laws or local ordinances. For a listing of other major firearms and related statutes, see **Appendix B**.

Firearms Transfer and Possession Eligibility

Under current law, there are nine classes of persons prohibited from shipping, transporting, receiving, or possessing firearms:

- persons convicted in any court of a crime punishable by imprisonment for a term exceeding one year;

- fugitives from justice;

- unlawful users or addicts of any controlled substance as defined in Section 102 of the Controlled Substances Act (21 U.S.C. §802));

- persons adjudicated as "mental defective" or committed to mental institutions;

- unauthorized immigrants and most nonimmigrant visitors (with some exceptions in the latter case);

- persons dishonorably discharged from the U.S. Armed Forces;

- persons who have renounced their U.S. citizenship;

- persons under court-order restraints related to harassing, stalking, or threatening an intimate partner or child of such intimate partner; and

- persons convicted of a misdemeanor crime of domestic violence.[35]

In addition, there is a 10th class of persons prohibited from shipping, transporting, or receiving firearms:

- persons under indictment in any court of a crime punishable by imprisonment for a term exceeding one year.[36]

Since 1994, moreover, it has been a federal offense for any non-licensed person to transfer a handgun to anyone younger than 18 years old. It has also been illegal for anyone younger than 18 years old to possess a handgun (there are exceptions to this law related to employment, ranching, farming, target practice, and hunting) (18 U.S.C. §922(x)).

Licensed Dealers and Firearms Transfers

Persons who are federally licensed to be engaged in the business of manufacturing, importing, or selling firearms are known as "federal firearms licensees (FFLs)." Under current law, FFLs may ship, transport, and receive firearms that have moved in interstate and foreign commerce. FFLs are currently required to verify with the FBI through a background check that non-licensed persons are eligible to possess a firearm before subsequently transferring a firearm to them. FFLs must also verify the identity of non-licensed transferees by inspecting a government-issued identity document (e.g., a driver's license).

---

[35] 18 U.S.C. §922(g).

[36] 18 U.S.C. §922(n).

FFLs may engage in interstate transfers of firearms among themselves without conducting background checks. Licensees may transfer long guns (rifles and shotguns) to out-of-state residents, as long as the transactions are face-to-face and not knowingly in violation of the laws of the state in which the unlicensed transferees reside. FFLs, however, may *not* transfer handguns to unlicensed out-of-state residents. Transfer of handguns by FFLs to anyone younger than 21 years old is also prohibited, as is the transfer of long guns to anyone younger than 18 years old (18 U.S.C. §922(b)). Also, FFLs are required to submit "multiple sales reports" to the Attorney General if any person purchases two or more handguns within five business days.

Furthermore, FFLs are required to maintain records on all acquisitions and dispositions of firearms. They are obligated to respond to ATF agents requesting firearms tracing information within 24 hours. Under certain circumstances, ATF agents may inspect, without search warrants, their business premises, inventory, and gun records.

Private Firearms Transfers

Non-licensees are prohibited from acquiring firearms from out-of-state sources (except for long guns acquired from FFLs under the conditions described above). Non-licensees are also prohibited from transferring firearms to any persons who they have reasonable cause to believe are not residents of the state in which the transaction occurs. In addition, since 1986 it has been a federal offense for non-licensees to knowingly transfer a firearm to prohibited persons. It is also notable that firearms transfers initiated through the Internet are subject to the same federal laws as transfers initiated in any other manner.[37]

Brady Handgun Violence Prevention Act

After seven years of extensive public debate, Congress passed the Brady Handgun Violence Prevention Act of 1993 (P.L. 103-159, the Brady Act)[38] as an amendment to the Gun Control Act of 1968, requiring background checks for firearms transfers between FFLs and non-licensed persons. The Brady Act included both interim and permanent provisions.

Interim Provisions

Under the interim provisions, which were in effect through November 1998, background checks were required for handgun transfers, and licensed firearms dealers were required to contact local chief law enforcement officers (CLEOs) to determine the eligibility of prospective customers to be transferred a handgun. The CLEOs were given up to five business days to make such eligibility determinations. Under the interim provisions, 12.7 million firearms background checks (for handguns) were completed during that four-year period, resulting in 312,000 denials.

---

[37] For further information, see CRS Report RS20957, *Internet Firearm Sales*, by T. J. Halstead.

[38] 107 Stat. 1536, November 30, 1993.

Permanent Provisions

On November 30, 1998, the Federal Bureau of Investigation (FBI) activated the National Instant Criminal Background Check System (NICS) to facilitate firearms-related background checks, when the permanent provisions of the Brady Act became effective.[39] Through NICS, FFLs conduct background checks on non-licensee applicants for both handgun and long gun transfers. The objective of a Brady background check is to ensure that an unlicensed transferee is not a prohibited person under the GCA.[40] It is notable that federal firearms laws serve as the minimum standard in the United States. States may choose, and have chosen, to regulate firearms more strictly. For example, some states require set waiting periods and/or licenses for firearms transfers and possession.

As part of a Brady background check, an FFL is required to submit a prospective firearm transferee's name, sex, race, date of birth, and state of residence through NICS. Social security numbers and other numeric identifiers are optional, but the submission of such data is likely to increase the timeliness of the background check (and reduce misidentifications).[41] The transferee's information is crosschecked against three computerized databases/systems to determine firearms transfer/possession eligibility. Those systems include the NICS index, Interstate Identification Index (III), and National Crime Information Center (NCIC).[42] If the transferee indicates that he is foreign born, his information is also checked against the immigration and naturalization databases maintained by the Department of Homeland Security, Immigration and Customs Enforcement.[43]

According to the FBI, the NICS index contains disqualifying records not found in either the III or NCIC on all the classes of prohibited persons enumerated in the GCA. It also includes records on persons previously denied firearms transfers. As of May 2010, the NICS index included a little over 6 million records.[44] The III, or "Triple I," is a computerized criminal history index pointer system that the FBI maintains so that records on persons arrested and convicted of felonies and serious misdemeanors at either the federal or state level can be shared nationally. All 50 states and the District of Columbia participate in the III, and the system holds indices to nearly 70 million criminal history records.[45] The NCIC includes files on information that is of immediate importance and applicability to law enforcement officials. Several NCIC files include over 4.4 million records on potentially prohibited persons. Hence, those files are pertinent to the Brady background check process. They include files on

---

[39] P.L. 103-159; November 30, 1993; 107 Stat. 1536.

[40] P.L. 90-618; October 22, 1968; 82 Stat. 1213; codified at 18 U.S.C. §921 et al.

[41] Querying Records in the System, 28 C.F.R. §25.7.

[42] Accessing Records in the System, 28 C.F.R. §25.6.

[43] Those databases include the Central Index System (CIS), Computer Linked Application Information Management System (CLAIMS), Deportable Alien Control System (DACS), National Automated Immigration Lookout System (NAIL II), Nonimmigrant Information System (NIIS), Student and Exchange Visitor Information System (SEVIS), Redesigned Naturalization Casework System (RNACS), Refugee, Asylum, and Parole System (RAPS), Enforcement Case Tracking System (ENFORCE), and the Treasury Enforcement Communications System (TECS).

[44] U.S. Department of Justice, *Report to Congress Pursuant to the NICS Improvement Amendments Act of 2007 (P.L. 110-180)*, July 1, 2010, Appendix C.

[45] Ibid., Appendix A.

- wanted persons (fugitives),

- persons subject to domestic abuse restraining orders,

- deported alien felons,

- persons in the U.S. Secret Service protective file,

- foreign fugitives, and

- known or suspected terrorists.

While the FBI handles background checks entirely for some states, other states serve as full or partial points of contact (POCs) for background check purposes. In POC states, FFLs contact a state agency, and the state agency contacts the FBI for such checks.[46]

As part of the Brady background check process, NICS will respond to an FFL or state official with a NICS Transaction Number (NTN) and one of three outcomes: (1) "proceed" with transfer or permit/license issuance, because a prohibiting record was not found; (2) "denied," indicating a prohibiting record was found; or (3) "delayed," indicating that the system produced information that suggested there could be a prohibiting record. Under the last outcome, a firearms transfer may be "delayed" for up to three business days while NICS examiners attempt to ascertain whether the person is prohibited.[47] At the end of the three-day period, an FFL may proceed with the transfer at his discretion if he has not heard from the FBI about the matter. The FBI, meanwhile, will continue to work the NICS adjudication for up to 90 days, during which the transaction is considered to be in an "open" status. If the FBI ascertains that the person is not in a prohibited status at any time during the 90 days, then the FBI will contact the FFL through NICS with a proceed response. If the person is subsequently found to be prohibited, the FBI will inform ATF and a firearms retrieval process will be initiated.

---

[46] In 13 states, state agencies serve as full POCs and conduct background checks for both long gun and handgun transfers. In four states, state agencies serve as partial POCs for handgun permits, whereas in another four states, state agencies serve as partial POCs for handgun transfers only. In these eight partial POC states, checks for long gun transfers are conducted entirely through the FBI. In the 30 non-POC states, the District of Columbia, and five territories (Guam, American Samoa, Northern Mariana Islands, Puerto Rico, and the Virgin Islands), FFLs contact the FBI directly to conduct background checks through NICS for both handgun and long gun transfers. For state agencies (POCs), background checks may not be as expeditious, but they may be more thorough because state agencies may have greater access to databases and records that are not available through NICS. According to the Government Accountability Office (GAO), this is particularly true for domestic violence misdemeanor offenses and protective orders. For further information, see GAO, *Gun Control: Opportunities to Close Loopholes in the National Instant Criminal Background Check System*, GAO-02-720, July 2002, p. 27.

[47] Accessing Records in the System, 28 C.F.R. §25.6.

Under no circumstances is an FFL informed about the prohibiting factor upon which a denial is based.[48] Under the Brady background check process, however, a denied person may challenge the accuracy of the underlying record(s) upon which his denial is based.[49] He would initiate this process by requesting (usually in writing) the reason for the denial from the agency that conducted the NICS check (the FBI or POC). The denying agency has five business days to respond to the request. Upon receipt of the reason and underlying record for the denial, the denied person may challenge the accuracy of that record. If the record is found to be inaccurate, the denying agency is legally obligated to correct that record.[50]

As with other screening systems, particularly those that are name-based, false positives occur as a result of Brady background checks, but the frequency of these misidentifications is unreported. Nevertheless, the FBI has taken steps to mitigate false positives. In July 2004, DOJ issued a regulation that established the NICS Voluntary Appeal File (VAF), which is part of the NICS Index (described above).[51] DOJ was prompted to establish the VAF to minimize the inconvenience incurred by some prospective firearms transferees (purchasers) who have names or birth dates similar to those of prohibited persons. So as not to be misidentified in the future, these persons agree to authorize the FBI to maintain personally identifying information about them in the VAF as a means to avoid future delayed transfers. Current law requires that NICS records on approved firearm transfers, particularly information personally identifying the transferee, be destroyed within 24 hours (see heading below, "Background Check Fee and Record Retention").

Under the GCA, there is also a provision that allows the Attorney General (previously, the Secretary of the Treasury) to consider petitions from a prohibited person for "relief from disabilities" and have his firearms transfer and possession eligibility restored.[52] Since FY1993, however, a rider on the ATF annual appropriations for salaries and expenses has prohibited the expenditure of any funding provided under that account on processing such petitions.[53] While a prohibited person arguably could petition the Attorney General, bypassing ATF, such an alternative has never been successfully tested. As a result, the only way a person can reacquire his lost firearms eligibility is to have his civil rights restored or disqualifying criminal record(s) expunged or set aside, or to be pardoned for his crime.

---

[48] Statement of Daniel D. Roberts, Assistant Director, Criminal Justice Information Services, Federal Bureau of Investigation, *Terrorists and Guns: The Nature of the Threat and Proposed Reforms: Hearing Before the S. Comm. on Homeland Sec. and Gov't Affairs*, 111th Cong., May 5, 2010.

[49] Correction of Erroneous System Information, 28 C.F.R. §25.10.

[50] Ibid.

[51] Final Rule, National Instant Criminal Background Check System Regulation, 69 *Federal Register* 43892 (July 23, 2004) (codified at 28 C.F.R. §25.10(g)).

[52] 18 U.S.C. §925(c). See also Relief from Disabilities Under the Act, 27 C.F.R. §478.144.

[53] For FY1993, see P.L. 102-393; 106 Stat. 1732 (1992). For FY2012, see P.L. 112-55; 125 Stat. 552, 609 (November 18, 2011). The FY2012 limitation provides: "That none of the funds appropriated herein shall be available to investigate or act upon applications for relief from Federal firearms disabilities under 18 U.S.C. 925(c)."

Table 4. Brady Background Checks for Firearms Transfers and Permits

1998-2009

Year	Total Annual Checks	Denials	FBI Checks	S&L Checks	FBI Denials[a]	POC Denials[b]
1998	893,127	18,647	507,000	386,127	8,836	9,811
1999	8,621,315	204,455	4,538,000	4,083,315	81,000	123,455
2000	7,698,643	153,087	4,260,270	3,438,373	66,808	86,279
2001	7,957,926	150,500	4,291,926	3,666,000	64,500	86,000
2002	7,805,792	135,973	4,248,893	3,556,899	60,739	75,234
2003	7,831,146	126,181	4,462,801	3,368,345	61,170	65,011
2004	8,083,809	125,842	4,685,018	3,398,791	63,675	62,167
2005	8,277,873	131,916	4,952,639	3,325,234	66,705	65,211
2006	8,612,201	134,442	5,262,752	3,349,449	69,930	64,512
2007	8,658,245	135,817	5,136,883	3,521,362	66,817	69,000
2008	9,900,711	147,080	5,813,249	4,087,462	70,725	76,355
2009	10,764,237	150,013	4,680,809	4,987,459	67,324	82,689
Total	95,105,025	1,613,953	54,242,859	40,862,166	748,229	865,724

Source: U.S. Department of Justice, Office of Justice Programs, Bureau of Justice Statistics, available at http://bjs.ojp.usdoj.gov/index.cfm?ty=pbse&sid=13.

Notes: On November 30, 1998, the interim provisions of the Brady Handgun Violence Prevention Act (P.L. 103-159) ended, and the permanent provisions were implemented when the FBI stood up the National Instant Criminal Background Check System (NICS).

a. In non-point of contact (non-POC) states, federal firearms licensees contact the FBI directly to conduct NICS background checks.

b. In point of contact (POC) states, federal firearms licenses contact a state agency and, in turn, the state agency contacts the FBI to conduct NICS background checks.

As shown in **Table 4**, under the permanent provisions of the Brady Act (December 1998 through 2009), more than 95.1 million checks were completed, resulting in more than 1.6 million denials, or nearly a 1.7% denial rate. More than 54.2 million of these checks were completed entirely by the FBI for non-point of contact (non-POC) states, the District of Columbia, and four territories. Those checks resulted in a denial rate of nearly 1.4%. Nearly 40.9 million checks were conducted by full or partial point of contact (POC) states.[54] Those checks resulted in a higher denial rate of 2.1%. **Table 5** shows breakouts for NICS denials by reasons and by denying agency.

---

[54] Ibid.

Table 5. Estimated Brady Background Check Denials

(1999 through 2009)

Reasons for denial	Total Denials	%	FBI Denials	%	State Denials	%	Local Denials	%
Felony indictment/conviction	904,904	56.1	482,608	64.5	387,491	52.8	34,806	26.4
State law prohibition	92,311	5.7	19,454	2.6	56,509	7.7	16,348	12.4
Domestic violence	237,323	14.7	119,717	16.0	99,808	13.6	17,798	13.5
Misdemeanor conviction	176,210	10.9	86,795	11.6	74,122	10.1	15,293	11.6
Restraining order	61,113	3.8	32,922	4.4	25,686	3.5	2,505	1.9
Fugitive	101,001	6.3	49,383	6.6	49,904	6.8	1,714	1.3
Illegal alien	13,322	0.8	9,727	1.3	2,936	0.4	659	0.5
Mental illness or disability	28,637	1.8	4,489	0.6	18,347	2.5	5,801	4.4
Drug user/addict	77,420	4.8	57,614	7.7	8,073	1.1	11,734	8.9
Local law prohibition	6,724	0.4	0		0		6,724	5.1
Other prohibitions	152,310	9.4	5,238	0.7	110,816	15.1	36,256	27.5
Totals^a	1,613,953	100.0	748,229	100.0	733,884	100.0	131,840	100.0

Source: U.S. Department of Justice, Office of Justice Programs, Bureau of Justice Statistics, *Background Checks for Firearms Transfers, 2009—Statistical Tables*, by Michael Bowling, et al., available at http://bjs.ojp.usdoj.gov/ index.cfm?ty=pbdetail&iid=2214.

a. Denials by reason subtotals are based upon percentages reported by BJS, which were applied to total denials by the FBI and state and local officials. Consequently, denials by reason may not sum precisely to the totals.

National Criminal History Improvement Program (NCHIP)

Under the Brady Act, Congress authorized a grant program known as the National Criminal History Improvement Program (NCHIP), the initial goal of which was to improve electronic access to firearms-related disqualifying records, particularly felony conviction records.[55] DOJ's Bureau of Justice Statistics (BJS) administers this program, under which grants are made to states to assist in updating and automating criminal history and other related records so that they are able to participate effectively in key federal criminal justice systems.[56] Besides the NICS Index, III, and NCIC, these systems also include the Integrated Automated Fingerprint Identification System (IAFIS) and the National Sex Offender Registry (NSOR).[57] This grant program is administered by BJS, which is part of the Office of Justice Programs.

---

[55] For further information, see Department of Justice, Office of Justice Programs, Bureau of Justice Statistics, *National Criminal History Program (NCHIP): Improving Criminal History Records for Background Checks, 2005*, July 2006.

[56] Ibid.

[57] Ibid.

Table 6. NCHIP Appropriations, FY1995 though FY2012

(dollars in millions)

Fiscal Year	Appropriation
FY1995	100.000
FY1996	26.500
FY1997	51.750
FY1998	47.750
FY1999	45.000
FY2000	35.000
FY2001	35.000
FY2002	38.000
FY2003	42.721
FY2004	32.634
FY2005	27.577
FY2006	12.796
FY2007	12.805
FY2008	12.220
FY2009	13.000
FY2010	14.500
FY2011	9.500
FY2012	6.000
Total	562.753

Source: U.S. Department of Justice, Office of Justice Programs, Bureau of Justice Statistics.

Table 6 shows that over the last 18 years (FY1995-FY2012), Congress has appropriated nearly $562.8 million for NCHIP, or an annual average of $31.3 million. Nevertheless, in 2007 congressional testimony following the April 16, 2007, Virginia Tech tragedy, DOJ reported that approximately half of the 70 million criminal history records in the Interstate Identification Index (III) were missing final dispositions—a circumstance that often results in delayed background checks and firearms transfers.[58] It was also reported that many states had not forwarded any records on persons adjudicated mentally defective to the FBI. As of April 30, 2007, the FBI reported that 22 states had contributed nearly 168,000 mental defective records to the FBI for inclusion in the NICS index;[59] however, other states had declined to report persons adjudicated mentally defective to the FBI. In many cases, state mental health, patients' rights, and privacy laws prohibited the disclosure of those records.[60] Other states may not have been able to report

[58] Statement of Rachel L. Brand, Assistant Attorney General for Legal Policy, Department of Justice at the Committee on Oversight and Government Reform Hearing on *Lethal Loopholes in Gun Purchase Laws*, May 10, 2007, p. 126.

[59] Ibid, p. 138.

[60] New York state, for example, had such a provision. See Section 33.13 of the Mental Health Law, which addresses the rights of patients and confidentiality of mental health records. Since enactment of P.L. 110-180, however, the New York State legislature addressed this issue and now provides mental defective records to the FBI for inclusion in the NICS Index.

such persons to the FBI because mental health "databanks" that would include such records are not maintained.[61] Following the Virginia Tech tragedy, the NICS mental defective file increased from 175,000 to 400,000 individual records, with California contributing more than 200,000 of those records.[62] By May 2010, that number had increased to more than 859,000 records, due in large part to NCIS Improvement Amendments Act (described below).[63] However, about half of the states had not contributed any records or had contributed only a handful of such records.[64]

For FY2012, the President's budget request included $12.0 million for NCHIP. The House-reported FY2012 Commerce-Justice-Science (CJS) appropriations bill (H.R. 2596) would have provided $6.0 million for NCHIP. The Senate-passed CJS appropriations bill (S. 1572) would have provided $8.0 million for this program. S. 1572 was folded into the Senate-passed FY2012 Minibus appropriations bill (H.R. 2112). The House- and Senate-passed conference report version of H.R. 2112 (H.Rept. 112-284), which the President has signed into law (P.L. 112-55), provides $6.0 million for NCHIP.

For FY2013, the Senate-reported CJS appropriations bill (S. 2323) would provide $6 million for NCHIP, the same amount as requested by the Administration. The House Committee on Appropriations ordered reported a similar measure that would provide the same amount for NCHIP.

NICS Act Record Improvement Program (NARIP)

Under the NICS Improvement Amendments Act of 2007,[65] Congress authorized the Attorney General to make additional grants to states to improve further electronic access to records, including court disposition and corrections records, that are necessary to fully facilitate NICS background checks. Under the act, the Attorney General is required to report annually to Congress on federal department and agency compliance with the act's provisions. Because BJS administers this program, the BJS Director is required to report annually on the progress that states are making in providing reasonable estimates of the number of firearms-related disqualifying records that they have jurisdiction over, as well as the number of those records that have been made accessible to the FBI for NICS background check purposes.[66] BJS has designated this grant program the "NICS Act Record Improvement Program (NARIP)," although congressional appropriations documents simply refer to it as "NICS improvement."

As shown in **Table 7**, Section 103(e) of the act included an authorization for appropriations for FY2009 through FY2013. The act directs that the grants provided under this authorization be made "in a manner consistent" with NCHIP. The act also requires that between 3% and 10% of each grant be allocated for a relief from disabilities program for persons adjudicated mentally

---

[61] Donna M. Norris, M.D., et al., "Firearms Laws, Patients, and the Roles of Psychiatrists," *American Journal of Psychiatry*, 163:8, August 2006, p. 1394.

[62] Dan Eggen, "FBI's Gun Ban Listing Swells: Thousands Added To File Marked 'Mental Defective,'" *Washington Post*, November 30, 2007, A01.

[63] U.S. Department of Justice, *Report to Congress Pursuant to Requirements of the NICS Improvement Amendments Act of 2007 (P.L. 110-180)*, July 1, 2010, Appendix C. Records Available in the NICS, as of May 10, 2010.

[64] Ibid.

[65] P.L. 110-180; January 8, 2008; 121 Stat. 2559.

[66] See U.S. Department of Justice, *Report to Congress Pursuant to the NICS Improvement Amendments Act of 2007 (P.L. 110-180)*, July 1, 2010.

defective. Also, as shown in **Table 7**, Section 301(e) of the act included an additional authorization for appropriations for the same fiscal years to improve state court computer systems to improve timeliness of criminal history dispositions. Under both authorizations, up to 5% of all grant funding may be set aside to provide assistance to tribal governments.

Table 7. NICS Improvement Authorizations and Appropriations under P.L. 110-180

(dollars in millions)

Fiscal Year	Section 103(e)	Section 301(e)	Actual Appropriation
FY2009	125	62.5	10.000
FY2010	250	125.0	20.000
FY2011	250	125.0	16.567
FY2012	125	62.5	5.000
FY2013	125	62.5	
Total	875	437.5	51.567

As an additional incentive, Section 102 of P.L. 110-180 also provides that on January 8, 2011, any state that provides at least 90% of disqualifying records is eligible for a waiver of the 10% match requirement under NCHIP for two years.[67] To be eligible for the waiver, as well as Section 103 grants, states are required to provide BJS with a reasonable estimate of the number of NICS-related disqualifying records that they hold within 180 days of enactment (July 6, 2008).

To further encourage compliance, Section 104 of P.L. 110-180 includes a schedule of discretionary and mandatory reductions in Byrne Justice Assistance Grants (JAGs)[68] for states that do not provide certain percentages of disqualifying records:

- for a two-year period (January 8, 2011, through January 8, 2013), the Attorney General may withhold up to 3% of JAG funding from any state that provides less than 50% of disqualifying records;

- for a five-year period (January 8, 2013, through January 8, 2018), the Attorney General may withhold up to 4% of JAG funding from any state that provides less than 70% of disqualifying records; and

- after January 8, 2018, the Attorney General is required to withhold 5% of JAG funding from any state that provides less than 90% of disqualifying records.

The Attorney General's assessments of a state's progress is to be based upon the reasonable estimates that the state itself is required to provide under the act for the purposes of implementing the Section 103 grants and the Section 102 NCHIP waiver (discussed above).[69] The act also

---

[67] For FY2005-FY2010, BJS invoked its discretionary authority to increase the match requirement to 20%. For FY2011, BJS reportedly reduced the match requirement to 10%, the percentage match requirement set out under the Crime Identification Technology Act (CITA; P.L. 105-251); CRS conversation with BJS on March 7, 2011.

[68] For further information, see CRS Report RS22416, *Edward Byrne Memorial Justice Assistance Grant (JAG) Program*, by Nathan James.

[69] As of July 1, 2010, 41 states and 1 territory had provided estimates to DOJ. As of December 31, 2009, 68 federal departments or agencies had also responded to a DOJ survey related to their obligations under P.L. 110-180. Twenty-
(continued...)

allows the Attorney General to waive the mandatory 5% cuts if a state provides substantial evidence that it is making reasonable compliance efforts.

Congress appropriated $10 million for NARIP in FY2009 and $20 million in FY2010. These amounts were well below the authorized levels in P.L. 110-180. In FY2009, BJS awarded $2.5 million in NARIP grants to the following grantees (individual amounts in parentheses):

- Nevada Department of Public Safety ($798,000),

- New York Division of Criminal Justice Services ($937,000), and

- Oregon State Police ($771,000).[70]

For FY2010, BJS awarded $16.9 million in NARIP grants to the following grantees (individual amounts in parentheses):

- Florida Department of Law Enforcement ($3.159 million),

- Idaho State Police ($1.950 million),

- Illinois State Police ($1.210 million),

- New Jersey Administrative Office of the Courts ($860,000),

- New York Division of Criminal Justice Services ($5.995 million),

- Oregon State Police ($2.0 million),

- Texas Department of Public Safety ($752,000), and

- Wisconsin Office of Justice Assistance ($981,000).[71]

To be eligible for NARIP grants, states must certify that they have established a relief from disabilities program for persons adjudicated to be mentally defective, whereby they can petition to have their gun rights restored. For FY2009, only 14 states submitted certification applications and only three were certified (Nevada, New York, and Oregon) and awarded grants. DOJ suggested that one factor that might have inhibited states from applying for NARIP grants is opposition at the state level to restoring firearm rights under any circumstance.[72] Another factor that might have influenced a state's choice is that NARIP funding only became available in March 2009, leaving little time to respond to the June 22, 2009, certification deadline.[73] Other

---

(...continued)

two reported possessing no disqualifying information. Twenty-three reported possessing secondary disqualifying information (e.g., employment background check investigative results). Ten agencies claimed to create and possess disqualifying information. And, ATF was reviewing those claims to determine whether that information was relevant to a NICS background check. Fourteen agencies needed further clarification from DOJ. See U.S. Department of Justice, *Report to Congress Pursuant to the NICS Improvement Amendments Act of 2007 (P.L. 110-180)*, July 1, 2010, pp. 5-6.

[70] U.S. Department of Justice, *Report to Congress Pursuant to Requirements of the NICS Improvement Amendment Act of 2007 (P.L. 110-180)*, July 1, 2010, p. 10.

[71] U.S. Department of Justice, Office of Justice Programs, Bureau of Justice Statistics, "NICS Improvement Amendments Act of 2007," http://bjs.ojp.usdoj.gov/index.cfm?ty=tp&tid=49.

[72] U.S. Department of Justice, *Report to Congress Pursuant to the NICS Improvement Amendments Act of 2007 (P.L. 110-180)*, July 1, 2010, p. 12.

[73] Ibid.

factors included budget constraints and the need to pass implementing legislation.[74] As shown above, eight states were awarded grants for FY2010. As of September 30, 2010, nine states had been certified.[75]

For FY2012, the President's budget request included $12.0 million for this program. The House-reported FY2012 CJS appropriations bill (H.R. 2596) would have provided $5.0 million for NARIP. The Senate-passed FY2012 CJS appropriations bill (S. 1572) would have provided $10.0 million for this program. S. 1572 was folded into the Senate-passed FY2012 Minibus appropriations bill (H.R. 2112). The House- and Senate-passed conference report version of H.R. 2112 (H.Rept. 112-284), which the President has signed into law (P.L. 112-55), provides $5.0 million for NARIP.

For FY2013, the Senate-reported CJS appropriations bill would provide $7.0 million for NARIP, or $2.0 million over the $5.0 million requested by the Administration. The House Committee on Appropriations ordered reported a similar measure that would provide $12.0 million for NARIP.

Background Check Fee and Record Retention

Beginning in FY1999, Congress has prohibited the collection of any fee for firearms-related background checks made through the FBI-administered NICS in DOJ appropriations.[76] Beginning in FY2004, that provision also included language to require the next-day destruction of approved background check records. The issue of approved Brady background check record retention has been contentious since the inception of the FBI-administered NICS, because a provision in the Brady Act (§103(i)) prohibits the establishment of any electronic registry of firearms, firearms owners, or approved firearms transactions and dispositions.

Nevertheless, under Attorney General Janet Reno DOJ proposed a rule on October 30, 1998, that would have allowed such records to be maintained for up to six months for audit purposes.[77] The NRA challenged this proposed rule in federal court, arguing that retaining the approved records was tantamount to a temporary registry. On July 11, 2000, the United States Court of Appeals for the District of Columbia found that nothing in the Brady Act prohibited the temporary retention of information about lawful firearms transfers for certain audit purposes.[78] On January 22, 2001, DOJ promulgated a final rule that allowed such records to maintained for up to 90 days.[79] Attorney General John Ashcroft opposed this rule, however, and DOJ proposed another rule on July 6, 2001, that called for the next-day destruction of those files.[80]

In July 2002, meanwhile, GAO reported that under Attorney General Reno, the FBI had conducted "non-routine" searches of the NICS audit log for law enforcement agencies to

---

[74] Ibid.

[75] CRS conversation with BJS on March 7, 2011.

[76] In the 110th Congress, the House-passed H.R. 2640 and Senate-reported S. 2084 include provisions that would permanently codify the NICS fee prohibition (see discussion of the NICS Improvement Amendments Act of 2007 above). For FY2012, such a prohibition is also included on an annual basis in the House-reported Commerce, Justice, Science Appropriations bill (H.R. 2596).

[77] 63 *Federal Register* 58303.

[78] *NRA* v. *Reno* (No. 99-5270, 216 F. 3d 122; 2000 U.S. App. Lexis 15906).

[79] 66 *Federal Register* 6470.

[80] 66 *Federal Register* 35567.

determine whether a person, whom subsequent information showed was a prohibited person, had been transferred a firearm within the previous 90 days. The FBI informed GAO that such searches were routinely conducted but were a "secondary benefit" given that the audit log was maintained primarily to check for system "accuracy, privacy, and performance." In addition, GAO reported that the next-day destruction of records would "adversely affect" other NICS operations, including firearms-retrieval actions, NICS audit log checks for previous background checks, verifications of NICS determinations for federal firearms licensees, and ATF inspections of federal firearms licensees' record keeping.[81]

Despite those adverse affects, opponents of greater federal gun control viewed the non-routine use of NICS records as being beyond the scope of authority given to the Attorney General under the Brady Act. GAO reported that DOJ took steps to minimize the adverse affects of the next-day destruction of those records. In the wake of the September 11, 2001, terrorist attacks, additional issues regarding Brady background checks emerged (see heading below, "Terrorist Watch List Screening and Brady Background Checks").

The Consolidated and Further Continuing Appropriations Act, 2012 (H.R. 2112), which the President has signed into law (P.L. 112-55), includes "futurity" language in the provision (§511) requiring that NICS approved firearm transfer records be destroyed within 24 hours. This "futurity" language makes the provision permanent law, as opposed to an annual appropriations restriction. Similar language was included in the House-reported FY2012 CJS appropriations bill (H.R. 2596). Senator Orrin Hatch offered several related amendments during Senate consideration of H.R. 2112, but the Senate ultimately did not vote upon those amendments.

Overview of Legislative Action in the 111th Congress

During the 111th Congress, the gun control debate was colored by two key Supreme Court decisions.[82] In *District of Columbia v. Heller*, the Court found that the District of Columbia (DC) handgun ban, among other regulations, violated an individual's right under the Second Amendment to lawfully possess a firearm in his home for self-defense. In *McDonald v. City of Chicago*, the Court found that an individual's right to lawfully possess a firearm for the purposes of self-defense under the Second Amendment applied to the states by way of the Fourteenth Amendment. Although the decision arguably limits a state's, city's, or local government's ability to prohibit handguns outright, it does not precisely delineate what would constitute permissible gun control laws under the Second Amendment. Consequently, these delineations will likely be developed in future cases.

In the 111th Congress, Members revisited several gun control issues that were previously considered in the 110th Congress. For example, some Members in the House of Representatives, who were dissatisfied with the District's response to the *Heller* decision, passed a bill in the 110th Congress that would have overturned provisions of the District's revised gun laws. In the 111th Congress, Members of the Senate amended and passed a DC voting rights bill (S. 160) with

---

[81] For further information on these issues, see GAO, *Gun Control: Potential Effects of Next-Day Destruction of NICS Background Check Records*, GAO-02-653, July 2002.

[82] For a legal analysis, see CRS Report R41750, *The Second Amendment: An Overview of District of Columbia v. Heller and McDonald v. City of Chicago*, by Vivian S. Chu.

similar language.[83] When the House turned its attention to DC voting rights, the leadership attempted to negotiate a compromise but ultimately tabled its version of the DC voting rights bill (H.R. 157) rather than risk amendments to overturn DC guns laws. The DC gun amendments were introduced as stand-alone bills (H.R. 5162/S. 3265). So far, the 112th Congress has not revisited this issue.

In the 111th Congress, the Senate Veterans' Affairs Committee reported stand-alone legislation that would have revamped procedures by which veterans are adjudicated "mentally incompetent" and, thus, lose their firearms possession and transfer eligibility (S. 669). This reported bill reflected an amendment that Senator Richard Burr had offered and the Senate committee had adopted in the 110th Congress during consideration of S. 2969. Also in the 111th Congress, the House Veterans' Affairs Committee considered a draft veterans' benefits bill and adopted an amendment offered by Representative John Boozman that included similar provisions. However, when the House considered the reported bill (H.R. 6132) under suspension of the rules, it was called to the floor without the Boozman provisions. As discussed below, this issue has reemerged in the 112th Congress, when the House passed similar legislation (H.R. 2349).

In the 111th Congress, the Senate also considered an amendment offered by Senator John Thune to the FY2010 Defense Authorization Act (S. 1390) that was narrowly defeated and arguably would have provided for national reciprocity between states regarding the concealed carry of firearms. In the 112th Congress, the House has passed similar legislation (H.R. 822). In addition, the Senate Committee on Homeland Security and Governmental Affairs held a hearing on denying firearms to persons watch-listed as known or suspected terrorists (S. 1317/H.R. 2159 and S. 2820). The 112th Congress revisited related issues during consideration of legislation to reauthorize the USA PATRIOT Act (H.R. 1800, S. 1038, and S. 990).

Several other legislative issues were considered in the 111th Congress that might remerge in the 112th Congress. For example, the House Financial Services Committee reported a bill (H.R. 3045; H.Rept. 111-277) that included a provision that would have prohibited public housing authorities from barring tenants from possessing legal firearms as a condition of their lease. This committee approved another housing bill that included a similar provision (H.R. 4868). The House also passed amendments (H.R. 5827) to federal bankruptcy law that would have allowed persons to claim either a single firearm or a collection of firearms of up to $3,000 in value as a federal exemption.[84] And, on at least two occasions, the Senate Committee on the Judiciary scheduled a hearing on a bill to reform federal statutes under which federally licensed firearms dealers are regulated (S. 941/H.R. 2296).

In the 111th Congress, Members sponsored several proposals that were enacted. The Senate adopted an amendment offered by Senator Tom Coburn to the Credit CARD Act of 2009 (H.R. 627) to allow people to carry firearms in national parks and wildlife refuges.[85] The House voted

---

[83] For further information, see CRS Report R40474, *DC Gun Laws and Proposed Amendments*, by Vivian S. Chu.

[84] For further information, see CRS Report R41799, *Exemptions for Firearms in Bankruptcy*, by Carol A. Pettit and Vastine D. Platte.

[85] Regarding public lands, the 112th Congress might consider additional proposals related to firearms carrying on public lands, such as water resources management projects (e.g., reservoirs at Corps-operated dams and inland waterways) managed by the Army Corps of Engineers or federal lands managed by the Bureau of Land Management (BLM). For related proposals in the 112th Congress, see the Recreational Self-Defense Act of 2011 (H.R. 1865/S. 1588) and the Recreational Shooting Act (H.R. 3440 and H.R. 4089). As described below, the House passed H.R. 4089 on April 17, 2012.

on the Coburn amendment as a separate measure and passed it as well (P.L. 111-24). The Senate also adopted an amendment offered by Senator Roger Wicker to the FY2010 Transportation-HUD appropriations bill (H.R. 3288) that allows private persons to carry firearms in their checked luggage on Amtrak trains. H.R. 3288 became the vehicle for the Consolidated Appropriations Act, 2010 (P.L. 111-117), which included the Wicker provision. Congress reconsidered and passed amendments to the Law Enforcement Officers Safety Act (LEOSA; P.L. 108-277) to clarify and widen eligibility for certain qualified police officers to carry concealed firearms across state lines (S. 1132; P.L. 111-272). Congress altered, but continued to make permanent, a funding limitation on the release of ATF firearms trace data (P.L. 111-8), which is known for its original sponsor, Representative Todd Tiahrt.

For the 111th Congress, gun trafficking across the Southwest border from the United States to Mexico was also an ongoing concern, as it has been for the 112th Congress.[86] The Consolidated Appropriations Act, 2010 (P.L. 111-117), included increased funding for ATF to investigate additional gun trafficking cases.[87] In addition, Congress provided ATF with an FY2010 supplemental appropriation to combat further Southwest border gun trafficking (P.L. 111-230). For a fuller discussion of legislative action in the 111th Congress, see **Appendix A**.

Emerging Issues in the 112th Congress

In the Consolidated and Further Continuing Appropriations Act, 2012 (H.R. 2112; P.L. 112-55), Congress included language that prohibits any funding provided under it from being expended to conduct investigations that allow firearms to be "walked." Revelations about ATF's conduct of a Phoenix, AZ-based Project Gunrunner investigation known as "Operation Fast and Furious" were the impetus for this language. The Attorney General has been questioned during several congressional hearings about who among the departmental officials conceived of, knew about, and/or approved this operation. It has led to the resignation of the U.S. Attorney for the District of Arizona. Several other gun control issues have emerged in the 112th Congress. For example, the House passed a bill (H.R. 822) that would establish greater reciprocity between states with firearms concealed carry statutes. The House also passed a Veterans Benefits bill (H.R. 2349) that would prohibit the Department of Veterans Affairs from making mentally incompetent determinations about beneficiaries for the purposes of gun control, unless such determinations were made by a judge, magistrate, or other judicial authority. Firearms-related amendments were also offered to bills that extended an expiring USA PATRIOT Act provision related to national security investigations and FBI access to business records. Moreover, the January 8, 2011, Tucson, AZ, shootings, in which Representative Gabrielle Giffords was severely wounded, have also prompted debate about the efficacy of several gun control proposals.

---

[86] For further information, see CRS Report R40733, *Gun Trafficking and the Southwest Border*, by Vivian S. Chu and William J. Krouse.

[87] For further information, see CRS Report RL34514, *The Bureau of Alcohol, Tobacco, Firearms and Explosives (ATF): Budget and Operations for FY2008, FY2009, and FY2010*, by William J. Krouse.

Concealed Carry and National Reciprocity[88]

The 112th Congress has revisited the issue of concealed carry and national reciprocity. On October 25, 2011, the House Committee on the Judiciary ordered reported the National Right-to-Carry Reciprocity Act of 2011 (H.R. 822) by a vote (19-11) that was nearly split down party lines following several days of contentious markup. On November 10, 2011, the committee reported H.R. 822 (H.Rept. 112-277). On November 16, 2011, the House considered and passed H.R. 822, amended, by a recorded vote: 272-154 (Roll no. 852).

H.R. 822 would establish an increased level of reciprocity among states that have laws that allow civilians to carry handguns in a concealed fashion. Under state law, 38 states, most recently Wisconsin, have enacted "shall issue" concealed carry laws, meaning permits are issued to all eligible applicants.[89] Ten states have enacted more restrictive "may issue" laws, meaning state and/or local authorities have discretion whether to issue permits.[90] In those states, applicants usually must demonstrate a need to carry a concealed handgun to the authorities. At one end of the spectrum, Alaska, Arizona, Wyoming, and Vermont allow concealed carry without a permit.[91] At the other end, Illinois and the District of Columbia allow no concealed carry of firearms by civilians.

With regard to interstate reciprocity, a handful of states have "recognition" statutes that recognize any state-issued concealed carry permit. Other states have "open" statutes that allow any resident of the United States, without regard to state residency, to apply for a concealed carry permit. Still other states have "hybrid" statutes that include elements of both the recognition and open statutes. Contiguous "shall issue" states often extend reciprocity to one another. However, some "shall issue" states have opted not to extend reciprocity to other "shall issue" states for a variety of reasons, even though they might have extended reciprocity to arguably more restrictive "may issue" states. The end result is a complicated array of state laws that arguably makes it very challenging for any individual to discern his legal ability to travel interstate with a concealed handgun.

Under H.R. 822, as ordered reported, a permit holder from state A would be able to travel to state B with a concealed handgun as long as state B had a concealed carry law, no matter which type ("shall" or "may" issue). The permit holder from state A would be required to comply with all other laws in state B, with the exception of the laws governing eligibility for and issuance of concealed carry permits. Several issues could arise, however. First, the bill makes no allowance for the difference between more permissive "shall issue" and more restrictive "may issue" state laws. Therefore, the bill could be viewed as an imposition by "shall issue" states over "may

---

[88] For additional information, see CRS Report R42099, *Federal Laws and Legislation on Carrying Concealed Firearms: An Overview*, by Vivian S. Chu.

[89] Wisconsin's concealed carry permit went into effect on November 1, 2011. "Shall issue" states include Alaska, Arizona, Arkansas, Colorado, Florida, Georgia, Idaho, Indiana, Iowa, Kansas, Kentucky, Louisiana, Maine, Michigan, Minnesota, Mississippi, Missouri, Montana, Nebraska, Nevada, New Hampshire, New Mexico, North Carolina, North Dakota, Ohio, Oklahoma, Oregon, Pennsylvania, South Carolina, South Dakota, Tennessee, Texas, Utah, Virginia, Washington, West Virginia, Wisconsin, and Wyoming.

[90] Alabama and Connecticut are "may issue" states that are considered to be more permissive than other "may issue" states. Those states include California, Delaware, Hawaii, Maryland, Massachusetts, New Jersey, New York, and Rhode Island.

[91] Alaska and Arizona issue permits to residents who seek to carry concealed firearms in other states that extend reciprocity to residents of Alaska.

---

issue" states. Depending upon the circumstances, the bill could also be viewed as an imposition by some "shall issue" states over other "shall issue" states, depending upon differences in their respective concealed carry laws. For example, some "shall issue" states have good moral character clauses as part of their eligibility requirements, others do not. Some require "live fire" training prior to permit issuance, others do not. Some require a mental health evaluation, others do not. Several states issue permits to persons 18 years of age, while most states require applicants to be 21 years of age.

Another issue that has emerged is "forum shopping," that is, one state's residents going to another state with an "open" statute so that they can return to their own state with a concealed carry permit that they would not have otherwise been able obtain in their own state. While language has been included in the bill, as ordered reported, that would arguably prevent individuals from forum shopping among states, Representative Daniel Lungren offered an amendment that the committee adopted that would require GAO to conduct a study of "open" state concealed carry laws and their implications for public safety.

The committee also adopted a substitute amendment offered by Representative Trent Franks at the outset of the markup. Twelve other amendments were offered, but all were defeated. Minority Members offered amendments that would have denied concealed carry permits to categories of persons on terrorist watch lists and several classes of misdemeanants, including sex offenders, stalkers, drug traffickers to minors, and assailants of police officers. Other amendments addressed the need for more secure and verifiable concealed carry documentation and interstate information sharing on permittees for law enforcement and public safety purposes. Representative Louie Gohmert offered an amendment that would have allowed concealed carry in the District of Columbia, but it too was defeated.

Proponents argue that establishing reciprocity on such a basis would be similar to the mutual recognition of out-of-state drivers licenses. Opponents counter that most state drivers license eligibility requirements are remarkably similar, unlike concealed carry eligibility requirements. Furthermore, states have opted to recognize the drivers licenses of other states largely on their own accord without congressional intervention. Proponents contend further that criminals are less likely to victimize individuals who could be armed, thus leading to a reduction in crime. To support this view, the chairman of the House Committee on the Judiciary, Representative Lamar Smith, noted during the markup that, according to the National Rifle Association (NRA), concealed carry states on average had lower violent crime rates (22%) than states that did not have such laws.[92] Opponents argue that introducing more firearms into potentially life threatening situations increases the likelihood that a firearm would be misused and innocent persons wounded or killed. To support their view, they have cited data compiled by the Violence Policy Center, which reported that from May 2007 through October 25, 2011, concealed carry permit holders had killed 11 law enforcement officers and 375 private citizens, and had engaged in 20 mass shootings and 29 murder/suicides.[93]

Several other concealed carry bills have been introduced in the House and the Senate. In the House, for example, Representative Paul Broun introduced the Secure Access to Firearms Enhancement Act (H.R. 2900), a bill that is similar in effect to the Thune bill (S. 2213) described

---

[92] According to the NRA, this lower average violent crime rate is based upon the FBI's 2004 Uniform Crime Reports data for only that year.

[93] Violence Policy Center, *Concealed Carry Killers*, http://www.vpc.org/ccwkillers htm.

below. Representative Timothy Johnson has introduced a bill (H.R. 3543) that has the same title as H.R. 822 and reflects that bill as introduced. Senator Barbara Boxer introduced the Common Sense Concealed Firearms Permit Act of 2011 (S. 176), which would facilitate concealed carry reciprocity arguably by establishing minimum federal eligibility requirements. On the other hand, elements of those eligibility requirements could be seen as being more restrictive than many existing state laws—particularly state "shall issue" laws. For example, the bill would require a concealed carry permit applicant to demonstrate (1) good cause for requesting the permit, and (2) that he is worthy of the public trust to carry a concealed firearm in public. Such eligibility requirements are arguably more closely aligned with state "may issue" laws. Senator Mark Begich introduced the National Right-to-Carry Reciprocity Act of 2012 (S. 2188), a companion bill to H.R. 822. And, Senator John Thune has introduced the Respecting States' Rights and Concealed Carry Reciprocity Act of 2012 (S. 2213). Under S. 2213, a resident of a state that allows concealed carry without a permit (Alaska, Arizona, Wyoming, and Vermont) would be allowed to do so in another state without a permit of any kind, arguably, as long the host state issues concealed carry permits. Under H.R. 822/S. 2188, a resident of one of those states would have to acquire a permit from either his or another state.

Firearms on Public Lands

The 112th Congress has revisited the issue of firearms carry and use on public lands. As described above, Senator Coburn sponsored legislation in the 111th Congress that allows individuals to carry firearms in national parks and wildlife refuges, as long as such firearms carry is in compliance with state and local laws (P.L. 111-24). On April 17, 2012, the House passed the Sportsmen's Heritage Act of 2012 (H.R. 4089) by a vote of 274-146 (Roll no. 164). This bill would prohibit any federal agency from banning recreational shooting on the public lands it manages. H.R. 4089 defines federal public lands broadly and, arguably, would promote allowance for hunting and shooting on most federal public lands, with certain exceptions for national parks, national monuments managed by the National Park Service, lands held in trust for Indian tribes, and Outer Continental Shelf lands. (For a related bill, see also H.R. 3440.) In addition, H.R. 4089 would prohibit the Environmental Protection Agency (EPA) from promulgating regulations under the Toxic Substances Control Act to restrict the lead content of ammunition and fishing tackle. The EPA was previously petitioned to address this issue on three occasions, but had denied those petitions. The EPA has adopted the position that it has no legal authority to regulate ammunition, and found that additional federal regulation of lead in fishing tackle is not warranted. (See also H.R. 1558/S. 838 and H.R. 2834/S. 2066.) Conversely, Representative Jim McDermott has introduced the Guns-Free National Parks Act of 2012 (H.R. 4063), a bill that would repeal the Coburn provision in P.L. 111-24 noted above.

On a related issue concerning firearms on public lands, Representative Bob Gibbs and Senator Jim Webb introduced the Recreational Land Self-Defense Act of 2011 (H.R. 1865/S. 1588). This bill would prohibit the Secretary of the Army from banning individuals from firearms possession, including an assembled or functional firearm, while traveling through or visiting water resources development projects (e.g., reservoirs at Corps-operated dams and inland waterways) managed by the Army Corps of Engineers. It is noteworthy that although Corps staff is often charged with maintaining order among boaters and other visitors at Corps-managed reservoirs and waterways, and at adjoining campsites, they are not authorized to be armed, unlike National Park Service rangers. Under the bill, however, firearms possession and carrying would still be subject to the state and local laws in effect for the jurisdictions in which the Corps projects are located. In this way, this bill is similar to the 2009 National Parks legislation (P.L. 111-24). Also, in the last session on July 14, 2011, the House passed an amendment (H.Amdt. 653) offered by Representative Paul Gosar to the FY2012 Energy and Water Development and Related Agencies Appropriations bill (H.R. 2354) that would have prohibited the expenditure of any funding under that bill to enforce any regulation to restrict firearms possession on corps projects or lands that exceeded state law.

ATF Southwest Border Gun Trafficking Investigations

Under Project Gunrunner, ATF has increased its efforts to staunch the flow of illegal guns from the United States to Mexico through stepped up enforcement of domestic gun control laws and cooperation with Mexican authorities. For example, ATF has trained Mexican law enforcement officials to use its eTrace program, through which investigators are sometimes able to trace the commercial trail and origin of recovered firearms and, in the process, identify gun trafficking trends and develop investigative leads. In November 2010, the DOJ Office of the Inspector General (OIG) released an evaluation of Project Gunrunner.[94] While the OIG was somewhat critical of ATF's eTrace program for yielding little "usable investigative leads,"[95] the OIG recommended that ATF work with DOJ to develop a reporting requirement for multiple long gun sales[96] because Mexican DTOs have demonstrated a marked preference for military-style firearms capable of accepting high-capacity magazines.[97] The OIG also recommended that ATF focus its investigative efforts on more complex criminal conspiracies involving high-level traffickers rather than on low-level straw purchasers.

ATF's Southwest border efforts to deter cross-border gun trafficking became controversial following the murder of a U.S. Border Patrol agent in December 2010. Firearms found at the murder site were linked to a Phoenix, AZ-based Project Gunrunner investigation known as "Operation Fast and Furious." This operation was an attempt by ATF's Phoenix field office to conduct a more complex investigation. However, allegations of misconduct on the part of DOJ's and ATF's upper-levels of management have been the topic of four hearings conducted by the House Committee on Oversight and Government Reform. Those allegations have also dominated the discourse at two DOJ oversight hearings held by the House Committee on the Judiciary, as well as two hearings held by the Senate Committee on the Judiciary and its Subcommittee on Crime and Terrorism. Several Members of Congress, including two House full committee chairs, have written letters to the Attorney General urging him and the Administration to be more forthcoming about possible missteps that were taken in the lead-up to Operation Fast and Furious. Besides the oversight issues, at issue for Congress is how widespread were the gun walking tactics employed? And, what can be done to prevent such gun walking tactics from being misused again, without unduly encumbering federal law enforcement?

Another related issue for Congress could be the Administration's arguably selective release of ATF firearms trace data. In the past, ATF periodically released data on firearms traces performed for Mexican authorities. Although substantive methodological limitations preclude using trace data as a proxy for the larger population of "crime guns" in Mexico or the United States, trace

---

[94] U.S. Department of Justice, Office of the Inspector General, *Review of ATF's Project Gunrunner*, I-2011-001, November 2010, http://www.justice.gov/oig/reports/ATF/e1101.pdf.

[95] Ibid, p. 73.

[96] Ibid, p. 40.

[97] Ibid, p. 38.

---

data have proven to be a useful indicator of trafficking trends and patterns.[98] In June 2009, GAO recommended to the Attorney General that he should direct ATF to regularly update its reporting on aggregate firearms trace data and trends.[99] For the next two years, nonetheless, only limited and arguably selected amounts of trace data were released by ATF. On April 26, 2012, ATF released updated but limited data on firearms trace requests that were processed for Mexican authorities.

Multiple Rifle Sales Report Proposal[100]

On December 17, 2010, DOJ and ATF published a "60-day emergency notice of information collection" in the *Federal Register*,[101] in which they requested that the Office of Management and Budget (OMB) review and clear a proposed information collection initiative by January 5, 2011, on an emergency basis under the Paperwork Reduction Act of 1995.[102] While ATF was not granted emergency approval, OMB eventually approved this initiative on July 11, 2011. While opponents responded quickly and passed a provision to block ATF's implementation of this initiative, the blocking provision was not included in ATF's enacted FY2012 appropriation and ATF is currently collecting multiple rifle sales reports in Southwest border states.

Under the initiative, ATF proposed to require federal firearms licensees (FFLs) to report to ATF whenever they make multiple sales or other dispositions of more than one rifle within five consecutive business days to an unlicensed person. Such reporting was to be limited to firearms that are (1) semiautomatic, (2) chambered for ammunition of greater than .22 caliber, and (3) capable of accepting a detachable magazine. While details underlying this initiative were not fully revealed in the *Federal Register*, on December 20, 2010, acting ATF Director Kenneth Melson later clarified that the proposed multiple rifle sales reporting requirement would be (1) limited to

---

[98] For FY2004 and every fiscal year thereafter, Congress has required ATF to include the following disclaimers in any published firearms trace reports: (a) Tracing studies conducted by the Bureau of Alcohol, Tobacco, Firearms, and Explosives are released without adequate disclaimers regarding the limitations of the data; (b) The Bureau of Alcohol, Tobacco, Firearms, and Explosives shall include in all such data releases, language similar to the following that would make clear that trace data cannot be used to draw broad conclusions about firearms-related crime: (1) Firearm traces are designed to assist law enforcement authorities in conducting investigations by tracking the sale and possession of specific firearms. Law enforcement agencies may request firearms traces for any reason, and those reasons are not necessarily reported to the Federal Government. Not all firearms used in crime are traced and not all firearms traced are used in crime. (2) Firearms selected for tracing are not chosen for purposes of determining which types, makes or models of firearms are used for illicit purposes. The firearms selected do not constitute a random sample and should not be considered representative of the larger universe of all firearms used by criminals, or any subset of that universe. Firearms are normally traced to the first retail seller, and sources reported for firearms traced do not necessarily represent the sources or methods by which firearms in general are acquired for use in crime; See §516 of the FY2012 Commerce, Justice, Science, and Related Agencies (CJS) Appropriations Act, which was enacted as part of the Consolidated and Further Appropriations Act, 2012 (P.L. 112-55).

[99] U.S. Government Accountability Office, *Firearms Trafficking: U.S. Efforts to Combat Arms Trafficking to Mexico Face Planning and Coordination Challenges*, GAO-09-709, June 2009, p. 59.

[100] This section was coauthored by the report's author, William J. Krouse, and Vivian S. Chu and Vanessa K. Burrows, CRS Legislative Attorneys. Questions on case law related to demand letters should be referred to Ms. Chu. Questions on the Paperwork Reduction Act (PRA) of 1995 should be referred to Ms. Burrows.

[101] Department of Justice, Bureau of Alcohol, Tobacco, Firearms and Explosives, "60-Day Emergency Notice of Information Collection Under Review: Report of Multiple Sale or Other Disposition of Certain Rifles," 75 *Federal Register* 79021, December 17, 2010.

[102] For further information, see CRS Report R40636, *Paperwork Reduction Act (PRA): OMB and Agency Responsibilities and Burden Estimates*, by Curtis W. Copeland and Vanessa K. Burrows.

FFLs operating in Southwest border states (Texas, New Mexico, Arizona, and California) and (2) confined initially to a one-year pilot project.[103]

On February 4, 2011, OMB informed ATF that it would not grant the emergency approval.[104] Nevertheless, the notice's 60-day comment period ran through February 16, 2011. Following DOJ and ATF consideration the initial round of comments, a subsequent 30-day comment period was invoked on April 29, 2010.[105] On July 11, 2011, OMB approved the information collection initiative for a three-year period (ending July 31, 2014).[106]

It appears that some of the impetus for the information collection initiative was a recommendation made by the DOJ OIG in November 2010.[107] As described above, in that review the OIG reported that ATF criminal investigations and firearms trace data indicated that Mexican drug trafficking organizations had demonstrated a marked preference for long guns (rifles and shotguns) capable of accepting detachable ammunition feeding devices.[108] As a consequence, the OIG recommended that ATF work with DOJ to explore options for seeking a multiple long sales reporting requirement.[109] In response to the OIG's recommendation, however, then Acting ATF Director Melson initially suggested that such a requirement could be beyond the ATF's and the DOJ's authority under current law, but that ATF would "explore the full range of options to seek information regarding multiple sales of long guns."[110]

Notwithstanding this concern about its authority, it appears that DOJ and ATF collectively concluded that there is sufficient authority under current law for ATF to collect reports on multiple sales of certain long guns from FFLs. Additional documentation posted on the OMB website suggested that ATF was proposing the information collection under its authority to issue "demand letters."[111] Since the enactment of the Gun Control Act (GCA) in 1968, the ATF and its predecessor agencies at the Department of the Treasury[112] have had the authority to issue "demand letters" to FFLs in order to obtain information from the records that FFLs are required by law to maintain at their places of business.[113] Such letters have been primarily used to investigate and bring non-compliant FFLs into line and to expedite the acquisition of trace data.[114]

---

[103] Bureau of Alcohol, Tobacco, Firearms and Explosives, "Acting Director Announces Demand Letters for Multiple Sales of Specific Long Guns in Four Border States," News Release, December 20, 2010.

[104] Mike Lillis, "House Dems Upset with Delay on Gun Proposal Along Border," *The Hill*, February 9, 2011, p. 3.

[105] Department of Justice, Bureau of Alcohol, Tobacco, Firearms and Explosives, "Agency Information Collection Activities; Proposed Collection Comments Requested: Report of Multiple Sale or Other Disposition of Certain Rifles," 76 *Federal Register* 24058, April 29, 2011.

[106] Office of Management and Budget, Office of Information and Regulatory Affairs, Reviews Completed in the Last 30 Days, DOJ-ATF, Report of Multiple Sale or Other Disposition of Certain Semi-Automatic Rifles, OMB Control Number: 1140-0100, http://www.reginfo.gov/public/do/PRAMain;jsessionid= 9f8e89cb30d6399089b4c8ac4da993b6c0e60ddbeff2.e34ObxiKbN0Sci0SbhaSa3aLchr0n6jAmljGr5XDqQLvpAe.

[107] U.S. Department of Justice, Office of the Inspector General, Evaluation and Inspections Division, *Review of ATF's Project Gunrunner*, I-2011-001, November 2010.

[108] Ibid, p. 40.

[109] Ibid.

[110] Ibid, p. 108.

[111] In a sample demand letter on the OMB website, ATF specified that it would be issuing such a letter under 18 U.S.C. §923(g)(5).

[112] ATF was transferred from the Department of the Treasury to the Department of Justice, effective January 2003. ATF was established in Treasury in 1972. Prior to that, it was a division within the Internal Revenue Service.

[113] The original demand letter regulation appears to have been promulgated at the same time the Gun Control Act was (continued...)

ATF's authority to issue demand letters to collect information under certain circumstances has been challenged and upheld in the federal courts. In 2000, for example, ATF issued demand letters to 41 FFLs who were deemed uncooperative because they had failed to comply with trace request responses in a timely manner. In these demand letters, the ATF required the FFLs to submit information concerning their firearm purchases and sales for the past three years and on a monthly basis thereafter until told otherwise.[115] The U.S. Court of Appeals for the Fourth Circuit held that 18 U.S.C. Section 926(a), which prohibits the creation of a national registry of firearms, firearms owners, and transactions, did not directly limit the defendant's authority to issue demand letters and was not violated because the ATF narrowly tailored the request to its tracing needs by issuing the letter to the 0.1% of FFLs nationwide.[116]

In 1999, the ATF sent out another demand letter to approximately 450 FFLs who had 10 or more crime guns traced to them with a "time-to-crime" of three years or less. The demand letter required the FFLs to report the acquisition of secondhand firearms, including identification of the firearm but not the identities of the person from whom the secondhand firearm was acquired or the person to whom the firearm was transferred.[117] The U.S. Courts of Appeals for the Fourth and Ninth Circuits generally held that Section 926(a) was not violated[118] and that the appropriations rider that prohibits ATF from spending money in connection with consolidating or centralizing records was also not violated because a demand letter sent to less than 1% of all FFLs for a portion of record information does not constitute consolidating or centralizing record information.[119]

Opponents of this initiative argue that (1) ATF does not enjoy sufficient authority to require multiple rifle sales reports from FFLs; (2) such a reporting requirement would be unprecedented; and (3) the data collection that would result would essentially constitute an illegal firearms registry. Although this information collection initiative would require FFLs to provide ATF with

---

(...continued)

enacted in 1968. See Furnishing Transaction Information, 27 C.F.R. §478.126, issued 33 *Federal Register* 18555, 18571, December 14, 1968. When the Firearms Owners' Protection Act (FOPA) was passed in 1986, Congress made explicit in statute: "Each licenses shall, when required by letter issued by the [Attorney General], and until notified to the contrary in writing by the [Attorney General], submit on a form specified by the [Attorney General], for periods and at the times specified in such letter, all record information required to be kept by this chapter or such lesser record information as the [Attorney General] may specify." See 18 U.S.C. §923(g)(5)(A).

[114] When considering FOPA, it seems that Congress made clear that although they would statutorily authorize the ATF to collect information pursuant to its demand letter authority, such authority "to request tracing information for dealers can never be used to establish any centralized or regional registration about §923(g)(5)(A) [in violation of §926(a)]" and "Congress had no intent to require all law-abiding gun dealers to report all their firearms transactions" to BATF. Statement of Senator Orrin Hatch, 131 *Congressional Record* S9129 (July 9, 1985).

[115] See RSM, Inc. v. Buckles, 254 F.3d 61,65-66 (4th Cir. 2001).

[116] Ibid, p. 68. The court in *RSM* noted that although FOPA prohibited the creation of a national registry of firearms, Congress also envisioned some sort of collection of firearms records so long as it was incidental to some other statutory function specifically delegated to ATF.

[117] See Blaustein & Reich, Inc. v. Buckles, 365 F.3d 281 (4th Cir. 2004); J&G Sales Ltd., v. Truscott, 473 F.3d 1043 (9th Cir. 2007), *cert. denied*, 128 S. Ct. 208 (2007).

[118] The Fourth Circuit in *Blaustein & Reich* noted that §926(a) has no bearing on the regulation that authorizes the use of demand letters because that section only prohibits the promulgation of rules and regulations prescribed after 1986, and the regulation on demand letters dates back to 1968. Furthermore, it stated that §926(a) has no bearing on §923(g)(5)(A) because "the former provision pertains only to 'rule[s]' and 'regulation[s]' and the latter is a statute, not a rule or regulation" (modification in the original). Blaustein & Reich, 365 F.3d at 288, 290.

[119] Blaustein & Reich, 365 F.3d at 289.

additional documentation on firearms transactions involving rifles, which has not previously been required, it is not entirely unprecedented. On the other hand, an argument could be made that ATF's issuance of demand letters and the existing multiple handgun sales reporting requirement are precedents for multiple rifle sales reports. In the past, as described above, ATF had administratively required some FFLs to surrender firearms transaction records temporarily on a much wider scale, when there were indications of noncompliance or illegal firearms trafficking.

Several Members of Congress, however, disagree with this decision and sent a letter to President Obama voicing strong opposition to the proposed multiple sales report proposal.[120] Those Members maintain that if Congress authorized multiple handgun sales reporting in statute in 1986, then it is incumbent upon ATF to request that Congress provide it with similar statutory authority for a multiple rifles sales reporting requirement.[121] On February 18, 2011, the House adopted an amendment by a roll call vote of 277-149 (Roll no. 115) offered by Representatives Dan Boren and Denny Rehberg to the Full-Year Continuing Appropriations Act, 2011 (H.R. 1) that would have prohibited ATF from implementing that requirement. While the House passed H.R. 1, the Senate rejected this bill on March 9, 2011, for budgetary considerations that went well beyond concerns about this policy rider. Meanwhile, the Department of Defense and Full-Year Continuing Appropriations Act, 2011 (H.R. 1473; P.L. 112-10) does not include a similar rider. Senator Jon Tester introduced a bill (S. 570) that would prohibit DOJ from collecting information on multiple rifle or shotgun sales.

Following OMB's approval of this information collection initiative, Representative Rehberg successfully amended the FY2012 Commerce-Justice-Science (CJS) appropriations bill (H.R. 2596) in full committee markup with language that would have prohibited ATF from implementing it by a vote of 25 to 16 on July 12, 2011. Meanwhile, the Senate folded its FY2012 CJS appropriations bill (S. 1572) into a minibus appropriations bill (H.R. 2112). Senator Dean Heller offered an amendment (S.Amdt. 843) to H.R. 2112 that would have also blocked implementation of the reporting requirement, but the Senate did not vote on the Heller amendment. Language reflecting the Rehberg amendment was not included in the House- and Senate-passed conference version of the Consolidated and Further Continuing Appropriations Act, 2012 (H.R. 2112). Hence, it was not included into the bill that was signed into law (P.L. 112-55) by the President on November 18, 2011. According to ATF, from August 14, 2011, through October 6, 2011, it collected 502 multiple rifle sales reports involving 1,276 firearms from FFLs in Southwest border states.[122]

This issue, however, has reemerged during the FY2013 appropriations cycle. On April 26, 2012, Representative Rehberg successfully offered an amendment during full committee markup of the CJS appropriations bill with language that would prohibit ATF from collecting multiple long gun sales reports. Representative Justin Amash and Senator Jon Tester have introduced similar proposals (H.R. 3814/S. 570)

Also, on April 26, 2012 (as described below), ATF released revised and updated trace data for calendar years 2007 through 2011. During the media briefing on trace data, ATF explained that so far less than 1,000 of the approximately 8,500 federally licensed gun dealers in Southwest border

---

[120] Congressional Documents and Publications, "Rehberg Leads Bipartisan Letter to ATF Questioning New Firearm Dealer Regulations," Representative Denny Rehberg (R-MT) News Release, December 23, 2010.

[121] Ibid.

[122] These statistics are available at http://www.atf.gov/statistics/.

states had been affected by the multiple rifle sales reporting requirement. Nevertheless, in the first six months those reports had generated approximately 28 case referrals to the U.S. Attorneys for prosecutions involving over 100 defendants.

Operation Fast and Furious

In February 2011, ATF and Project Gunrunner came under congressional scrutiny for a Phoenix, AZ-based investigation known as Operation Fast and Furious.[123] ATF whistleblowers have alleged that suspected straw purchasers were allowed to amass relatively large quantities of firearms as part of long-term gun trafficking investigations.[124] As a consequence, some of these firearms are alleged to have "walked," meaning that they were trafficked to gunrunners and other criminals before ATF moved to arrest the suspects and seize all of their contraband firearms.[125] Some of these firearms were reportedly smuggled into Mexico.[126] Two of these firearms—AK-47 style rifles—were reportedly found at the scene of a shootout near the U.S.-Mexico border where U.S. Border Patrol Agent Brian Terry was shot to death.[127] Press accounts assert that ATF has acknowledged that as many as 195 firearms that were purchased by persons under ATF investigation as part of Operation Fast and Furious were recovered in Mexico.[128] Questions, moreover, have been raised about whether a firearm—an AK-47 style handgun—that was reportedly used to murder U.S. ICE Special Agent Jamie Zapata and wound Special Agent Victor Avila in Mexico on February 15, 2011, was initially trafficked by a subject of a Houston, TX-based ATF Project Gunrunner investigation.[129]

U.S. and Mexican policymakers have expressed their dismay over the circumstances surrounding Operation Fast and Furious.[130] Senator Charles E. Grassley, the ranking minority Member on the Senate Judiciary Committee, wrote several letters to ATF and U.S. Attorney General Eric H. Holder voicing his concerns about Operation Fast and Furious and the whistleblower allegations that were brought to him. Attorney General Holder instructed the DOJ OIG to review ATF's gun trafficking investigations.[131] On March 8, 2011, however, Senator Grassley called for an independent review of the related allegations because the DOJ OIG had made recommendations about Southwest border gun trafficking investigations in its November 2011 audit that might possibly influence its future findings.[132]

---

[123] James V. Grimaldi and Sari Horwitz, "ATF Probe Strategy Is Questioned," *Washington Post*, February 2, 2011, p. A04.

[124] Ibid.

[125] Ibid.

[126] John Solomon, David Heath, and Gordon Witkin, "ATF Let Hundreds of U.S. Weapons Fall Into Hands of Suspected Mexican Gunrunners: Whistleblower Says Agents Strongly Objected to Risky Strategy," *Center for Public Integrity*.

[127] Ibid.

[128] Kim Murphy and Ken Ellingwood, "Mexico Demands Answers on Guns," *Chicago Tribune*, March 11, 2011, p. 13.

[129] Ibid.

[130] Ken Ellingwood, "Mexico: U.S. Never Said Guns Came Across; Washington Didn't Reveal Tracked Arms Were Passing the Border, Agency Asserts," *Los Angeles Times*, March 12, 2011.

[131] Pete Yost, "Justice IG to Look into Anti-Gun Efforts on Border," *Associated Press Online*, March 4, 2011.

[132] James V. Grimaldi, "ATF Faces Federal Review Over Tactics to Foil Gunrunning Rings," *Washington Post*, March 10, 2011, p. A04.

On March 9, 2011, Representative Lamar Smith, chair of the House Judiciary Committee, wrote the Attorney General and commended him for tasking the OIG with a review of ATF's firearms trafficking investigatory methods. In addition, Representative Smith asked DOJ to respond to the following questions by March 18, 2011:

- "How many weapons have been allowed to pass to Mexico under the program known as "Fast and Furious"? Is the program still active?

- Who at ATF Headquarters approved the program?

- Who in the U.S. Attorney's Office for the District of Arizona approved the program? On what authority did the office approve the program?

- Did ATF or the U.S. Attorney's Office in Phoenix coordinate the "Fast and Furious" program with the Department of Justice? Did the department approve the strategy?

- What changes or improvements has ATF made to its eTrace program and its ability to use intelligence to target gun trafficking organizations in general?

- Does ATF view the "Fast and Furious" program as a success?"

DOJ responded to Representative Smith to say that the matter was under investigation. On April 1, 2011, Representative Darrell Issa, chairman of the House Oversight and Government Reform Committee, issued a subpoena to DOJ and ATF for documents related to Project Gunrunner following several unanswered requests for information related to ATF's anti-gun trafficking efforts on the Southwest Border.[133]

On June 14, 2011, Representative Issa and Senator Grassley issued a joint staff report on Operation Fast and Furious,[134] which chronicled that ATF line supervisors became increasingly concerned when they witnessed hundreds of firearms being illegally transferred during surveillance operations, but they were reportedly directed not to arrest the suspects and interdict those firearms. Those agents contend that this was a questionable departure from past investigative practices. On June 15, 2011, the House Committee on Oversight and Government Reform held a hearing on these matters. Representative Issa, chairman of the committee, expressed his concern that DOJ had not been entirely cooperative with his committee's efforts to investigate how some of those firearms found their way to crime scenes in Mexico and on the Southwest border.

Following the hearing, on June 29, 2011, Representative Elijah E. Cummings, the committee's ranking minority Member, issued a report and held a forum during which the minority explored issues raised by some of those same ATF line supervisors, who had suggested during the House hearing that the penalties for firearm straw purchases under current law are arguably not stringent enough. The minority also discussed other gun control proposals related to gun shows,

---

[133] Press Release, "Chairman Issa Subpoenas ATF for 'Project Gunrunner' Documents," April 1, 2011.

[134] U.S. Congress, Joint Staff Report, *Department of Justice's Operation Fast and Furious: Accounts of ATF Agents*, prepared for Representative Darrell E. Issa, Chairman, United States House of Representatives, Committee on Oversight and Government Reform, and Senator Charles E. Grassley, Ranking Member, United States Senate, Committee on the Judiciary, 112th Cong., 1st sess., June 14, 2011, http://oversight house.gov/images/stories/Reports/ATF_Report.pdf.

semiautomatic assault weapons, sniper rifles, and additional penalties for gun trafficking offenses.[135]

On July 26, 2011, the House Committee on Oversight and Government Reform held a follow-up hearing on Operation Fast and Furious. As preceded the earlier hearing, a joint staff report was issued.[136] This report found that ATF and DOJ leadership had not informed its own Attaché serving in Mexico City, the U.S. Ambassador to Mexico, nor the Mexican authorities about the investigation.[137] As recovered firearms in Mexico increased, the ATF Attaché in Mexico City became more alarmed and contacted his superiors at ATF headquarters to express his grave concerns about the implications that this increased flow of illegal firearms could have for both Mexican and U.S. law enforcement officers as well as the public on both sides of the border. He and others were told by both ATF and DOJ officials that the investigation was under control and was having positive results.[138] As noted above, however, Border Patrol Agent Terry was killed in a firefight in December 2010, and firearms connected to Operation Fast and Furious were found at the site of that firefight.

In July 2011, the *Washington Post* reported that Operation Fast and Furious ultimately involved 2,020 firearms, of which 227 had been recovered in Mexico and 363 had been recovered in the United States.[139] The investigation resulted in indictments of 20 individuals on multiple counts of straw purchasing and other federal offenses.[140] While ATF officials maintained that the investigation had yet to be concluded and additional arrests of "high-level traffickers" might be forthcoming,[141] no additional arrests have been made.

As called for originally by Senator Grassley, the House Appropriations Committee included report language with the Commerce-Justice-Science (CJS) appropriations bill (H.R. 2596; H.Rept. 112-169) that recommended the appointment of "an outside, independent investigator," who would be charged with conducting "a thorough investigation of the allegations against ATF with respect to Operation Fast and Furious and policies guiding this and similar operations." In addition, the House committee called on both DOJ and ATF to cooperate fully with related oversight investigations, whether they were conducted by congressional committees, the DOJ OIG, or an independent investigator. Conversely, the Senate Appropriations Committee included report language with the CJS appropriations bill (S. 1572; S.Rept. 112-78) that stated that the OIG would fulfill its oversight duties, and that Operation Fast and Furious was but a small part of

[135] U.S. Congress, House Oversight and Government Reform Committee, Minority Staff Report, *Outgunned: Law Enforcement Agents Warn Congress They Lack Adequate Tools to Counter Illegal Firearms Trafficking*, 112th Cong., 1st sess., June 30, 2011, http://democrats.oversight house.gov/images/stories/ OUTGUNNED%20Firearms%20Trafficking%20Report%20-%20Final.pdf. On July 15, 2011, Representative Carolyn B. Maloney introduced the Stop Gun Trafficking and Strengthen Law Enforcement Act of 2011 (H.R. 2554). Original cosponsors included Representative Cummings and Representative Carolyn McCarthy.

[136] U.S. Congress, Joint Staff Report, *Department of Justice's Operation Fast and Furious: Fueling Cartel Violence*, prepared for Representative Darrell E. Issa, Chairman, United States House of Representatives, Committee on Oversight and Government Reform and Senator Charles E. Grassley, Ranking Member, United States Senate, Committee on the Judiciary, 112th Cong., 1st sess., July 26, 2011.

[137] Ibid, p. 27.

[138] Ibid.

[139] Sari Horwitz, "A Gunrunning Sting Gone Fatally Wrong: Operation Meant to Seize Firearms Bound for Cartels Allows Weapons into the Streets," *Washington Post*, July 26, 2011, p. A1.

[140] Ibid.

[141] Ibid.

ATF's Southwest border operations, which should not detract from the agency's efforts to protect Americans from illegal gun trafficking and other forms of cross-border crime. Conference report language accompanying the Consolidated and Further Appropriations Act, 2012 (H.R. 2112; P.L. 112-55) does not call for an independent investigator, but it does call on both DOJ and ATF to cooperate fully with congressional oversight efforts (H.Rept. 112-284, p. 240).

On August 30, 2011, among the fallout from Operation Fast and Furious, U.S. Attorney for the District of Arizona Dennis K. Burke resigned[142] and ATF Acting Director Melson was reassigned to the DOJ Office of Legal Policy.[143] In Melson's place, U.S. Attorney for the District of Minnesota B. Todd Jones was appointed interim acting ATF Director.[144] However, Jones is not President Obama's nominee for ATF Director.[145] The President's nominee remains Andrew Traver, the ATF Chicago Special Agent in Charge.[146]

On September 23, 2011, Representative Smith sent Attorney General Holder a second letter expressing his continuing concerns about Operation Fast and Furious, as well as the appointment of an acting ATF director who would be focused on both his duties as ATF acting director and U.S. Attorney for the District of Minnesota. He noted a provision in the FY2010 Omnibus Appropriations Act (P.L. 111-117) requires each U.S. Attorney to reside in the district in which he serves, and questioned how Jones would be able to serve simultaneously in Minnesota as U.S. Attorney and Washington as ATF acting director. As a follow-up to his March 9 letter, Representative Smith asked DOJ to respond to the following questions by October 21, 2011:

- "Is the Department considering additional staff changes at ATF in response to *Operation Fast and Furious*?

---

[142] Jerry Markon and Sari Horwitz, "ATF Head Removed Amid Furor Over Guns," *Washington Post*, August 31, 2011, p. A01.

[143] U.S. Department of Justice, Department of Justice Announces New Acting Director of ATF and Senior Advisor in the Office of Legal Policy, press release, August 30, 2011.

[144] Ibid.

[145] Sari Horwitz, "Trying to Steady a Shaken ATF: Acting Director Hopes to Rebuild Morale After Fury Over Tactics in Gun-Trafficking Operation," *Washington Post*, September 2, 2011, p. A16.

[146] Section 504 of the USA PATRIOT Improvement and Reauthorization Act of 2005 (P.L. 109-177; March 9, 2006; 120 Stat. 247) requires the ATF Director to be appointed by the President with the advice and consent of the Senate. The position of ATF Director, however, has not been filled permanently since August 2006, after ATF Director Carl J. Truscott resigned due to preliminary findings by the DOJ OIG that he had engaged in questionable expenditures and management practices while serving as ATF Director. In September 2006, President George W. Bush appointed the U.S. Attorney for the District of Boston, Michael J. Sullivan, acting ATF Director. Sullivan served in both posts concurrently. In February 2008, his confirmation as ATF Director was blocked in the Senate, when several Senators voiced their concern about ATF's "overly aggressive" enforcement of gun laws and the nominee's views on such matters. Sullivan resigned as acting ATF Director on January 20, 2009. Ronnie Carter served as acting Director until April 2009, when Kenneth Melson was appointed acting Director. In November 2009, Melson was appointed acting Deputy Director, because the 210-day statutory limit on the acting Director's tenure had expired. On November 17, 2010, the Obama Administration nominated Andrew Traver, the ATF Special Agent in Charge in Chicago, to be ATF Director. Because the Senate did not act on this nomination in the 111th Congress, Traver was renominated by the Administration on January 5, 2011. See U.S. Department of Justice, Office of the Inspector General, Oversight and Review Division, *Report of Investigation Concerning Alleged Mismanagement and Misconduct by Carl J. Truscott, Former Director of the Bureau of Alcohol, Tobacco, Firearms and Explosives* (October 2006). Jonathan Saltzman, "Sullivan ATF Confirmation Blocked; La. Senator Objects to Gun-License Stance," *Boston Globe*, February 14, 2008, p. B1. Jonathan Saltzman, "US Attorney To Resign Sooner Than Expected: List of Finalists for Post Not Yet Sent To Obama," *Boston Globe*, April 16, 2009, p. 2. Andrew Ramanos, "Senate Returns ATF Nomination to White House," *Main Justice: Politics, Policy and the Law*, December 23, 2010. The White House, Office of the Press Secretary, "Presidential Nominations Sent to the Senate," January 5, 2011.

- How does the Department justify accepting the resignation of the U.S. Attorney while the ATF's managers in charge of *Fast and Furious* appear to have faced no discipline?

- What role did the Department play in oversight of *Operation Fast and Furious*?

- Does Todd Jones intend to maintain his residence in Minnesota while serving as acting director of ATF?

- Is the Department confident that the ATF can fulfill its mission with a part-time director who is based in Minnesota?

- Have you issued a waiver of the residency requirement for Todd Jones under 28 U.S.C. §545? If so, for what period does the waiver extend?"

In addition, Representative Smith reiterated his concern about how the department had responded to congressional inquiries about Operation Fast and Furious. He noted for the record that the department had only answered one out of six questions he submitted in his March 9 letter. He raised concerns about what appeared to be deliberate attempts by the department to obscure the facts about Operation Fast and Furious. As an example, Representative Smith raised the department's description of the ballistic tests on the two semiautomatic rifles found at the site of Border Patrol Agent Terry's murder. The department apparently stated that the tests showed that neither firearm was used to fire the fatal shot; however, Representative Smith countered that the tests were inconclusive one way or another. Furthermore, Representative Smith raised an issue about an audio recording on which a federal agent reportedly mentioned a third firearm linked to Operation Fast and Furious that had been found at Agent Terry's murder scene.

On October 12, 2011, the Committee on Oversight and Government Reform issued a subpoena to DOJ for all departmental communications and documents "referring or related to Operation Fast and Furious, the Jacob Chambers Case, or any Organized Crime Drug Enforcement Task Force (OCDETF) firearms trafficking cases based in Phoenix, Arizona."[147] According to a press release, Representative Issa said, "The documents this subpoena demands will provide answers to questions that Justice officials have tried to avoid [answering] since this investigation began eight months ago."[148] On October 16, 2011, Representative Issa and Sharyl Attkisson—the CBS correspondent who broke the Operation Fast and Furious story nationally—appeared on *Face the Nation* with Bob Schieffer.[149] Both Representative Issa and Ms. Attkisson discussed the possibility that a third firearm had been found at Agent Terry's murder scene. According to Ms. Attkisson, audio recordings had surfaced on which the ATF supervisory special agent in charge of Operation Fast and Furious made mention of a third firearm, an SKS rifle, that was possibly linked to a confidential informant working for either the FBI or DEA.[150] Representative Cummings has called on the Committee on Oversight and Government Reform to hear testimony

---

[147] U.S. House of Representatives, Committee on Oversight and Government Reform, "Oversight Committee Subpoenas Attorney General for 'Operation Fast and Furious' Communications and Documents," Press Release, October 18, 2011, http://oversight.house.gov/index.php?option=com_content&view=article&id=1479:oversight-committee-subpoenas-attorney-general-for-operation-fast-and-furious-communications-and-documents-&catid=22:releasesstatements.

[148] Ibid.

[149] CBS News, "Face the Nation" Transcript: October 15, 2011, http://www.cbsnews.com/8301-3460_162-20121072/face-the-nation-transcript-october-16-2011/.

[150] Ibid.

---

again from former ATF Acting Director Melson as a means of determining who is responsible for the conduct of this controversial gun trafficking operation.[151]

On October 18, 2011, Senator John Cornyn offered an amendment (S.Amdt. 775) to the FY2012 minibus appropriations bill (H.R. 2112), which included the Senate-reported FY2012 CJS appropriations bill (S. 1572), to prohibit the expenditure of any funding provided under that bill, if enacted, to conduct criminal investigations that allowed firearms to be transferred *knowingly* to agents of drug cartels and U.S. law enforcement was unable to continuously monitor *or* control such firearms at all times. This amendment passed 99-0 (Record Vote Number: 167). On November 1, 2011, the Senate passed H.R. 2112. The conference report version of H.R. 2112 (H.Rept. 112-284), which both the House and Senate passed and the President signed into law (P.L. 112-55), includes a modified version of the Senate-passed Cornyn amendment. The modified provision (§219) prohibits the expenditure of any funding provided under P.L. 112-55 to be used by a federal law enforcement officer to transfer an operable firearm to a person suspected or known to be connected to a drug cartel without that firearm being continuously monitored or controlled.

On November 1, 2011, Lanny Breuer, the Assistant Attorney General for DOJ's Criminal Division, testified before the Senate Judiciary's Crime and Terrorism Subcommittee at a hearing on International Organized Crime.[152] During the hearing, Senator Grassley acknowledged a statement made by Breuer on the previous day regarding a 2006-2007 Phoenix-based ATF investigation known as Operation Wide Receiver. With regard to that operation, Breuer said he first became aware of the "gun walking" strategy in April 2010, and it concerned him. However, he did not take his concerns about "gun walking" directly to the Attorney General. Instead, his subordinate spoke to "ATF leadership" about his concerns. Breuer testified that about 350 firearms were allowed to "walk" as part of Operation Wide Receiver, but he failed to make possible connections between Operation Wide Receiver and Operation Fast and Furious with regard to "gun walking." Nevertheless, in his October 31, 2011, statement, Breuer characterized "gun walking" as "unacceptable and misguided."[153] Breuer also testified that over the past nearly five-year period, ATF had processed 94,000 firearm trace requests for Mexican authorities. Of those firearms, 64,000 were "traced" to the United States. In addition, on November 4, 2011, the *Huffington Post* reported that nearly 700 firearms linked to Operation Fast and Furious had been recovered: 276 in Mexico and 389 in the United States, according to ATF data through October 20, 2011.[154]

On November 8, 2011, the Senate Committee on the Judiciary held a DOJ oversight hearing, at which Senators Grassley and Cornyn questioned Attorney General Holder at length about Operation Fast and Furious. The Attorney General conceded that a February 4, 2011, letter from DOJ to congressional investigators contained "inaccurate" information regarding the depth of knowledge that departmental officials had of ATF's use of the "gun walking" tactic.[155] In addition,

---

[151] "Cummings Responds to Issa's Accusations of FBI Evidence Tampering," *States News Service*, October 17, 2011.

[152] *Combating International Organized Crime: Evaluating Current Authorities, Tools, and Resources: Hearing before the Senate Committee on the Judiciary, Subcommittee on Crime and Terrorism*, 112th Congress, November 1, 2011 (CQ Congressional Transcripts).

[153] U.S. Department of Justice, *Assistant Attorney General Lanny Breuer Issues Statement On 'Operation Wide Receiver'*, October 31, 2011.

[154] Pete Yost, "Fast and Furious-Like 'Gun-Walking' Probe Mentioned In 2007 Bush Administration Memo," *Huffington Post*, November 4, 2011.

[155] Jerry Jarkon, "Holder Amends remarks On Gun Sting: Attorney General Heard of 'Fast and Furious' Earlier Than (continued...)

---

the Attorney General qualified Breuer's earlier statement about 64,000 firearms recovered in Mexico having been "traced" back to the United States. As described below, only about a quarter of the 94,000 firearms submitted for tracing were probably ever fully traced back to the first U.S. retail owner of record. Consequently, the Attorney General stated that 64,000 of those firearms were "sourced" to the United States, in that they were either originally manufactured in, or imported into, the United States. However, no additional information was given about the 25,000 or so firearms that were eventually fully traced back to the United States, such as time-to-recovery or most frequently traced firearms (by type, make, model, and caliber).

On December 8, 2011, the House Committee on the Judiciary held a hearing on DOJ oversight and heard testimony from Attorney General Holder. However, Operation Fast and Furious was clearly the predominant issue before the committee.[156] More specifically, at issue was what levels of management within DOJ had knowledge and, by extension, responsibility for where the operation lay. For example, at a May 3, 2011, DOJ oversight hearing, Attorney General Holder testified that he had only heard about Operation Fast and Furious "over the last few weeks."[157] On the other hand, internal DOJ documents obtained by the House Oversight and Government Reform Committee suggest that several high-level managers within the department were aware of, and possibly helped direct, ATF's Operation Fast and Furious.[158] There were also emails between William Newell, the then-ATF Phoenix Special Agent in Charge, and at least one staff member of the National Security Council in which "updates" on Operation Fast and Furious were provided.[159] On January 31, 2012, Chairman Smith sent the Attorney General a third letter, in which he admonished DOJ's stalling tactics and selective releases of materials related to the operation. In the letter, he surmised that "It is past time for the Department to provide a full and honest accounting of Operation Fast and Furious with details about its conception, approval, and who knew what when."[160]

On February 2, 2012, the House Oversight and Government Reform Committee held its fourth hearing related to Operation Fast and Furious, during which Attorney General Holder was questioned at length about possible false statements, and other questionable responses to repeated congressional inquiries, that were made with regard to this operation by the department. As a counterpoint, Representative Cummings noted that his staff had prepared a report that documented that "gun walking" operations had been conducted by the ATF and U.S. Attorneys' Phoenix offices as part of several Southwest border gun trafficking investigations.[161] In addition

---

(...continued)

He First Said," *Washington Post*, November 9, 2011, p. A2.

[156] *Oversight of the Department of Justice: Hearing before the House Committee on the Judiciary*, 112th Congress, December 8, 2011 (CQ Congressional Transcripts).

[157] *Oversight Hearing on the United States Department of Justice: Hearing before the House Committee on the Judiciary*, 112th Congress, May 3, 2011 (CQ Congressional Transcripts).

[158] Press release, "Issa to Holder: 'You Own Fast and Furious," October 10, 2011, http://oversight.house.gov/ index.php?option=com_content&task=view&id=1474&Itemid=29. See also, Jackie Hicken, "All Eyes on Holder as Memos Suggest He Knew More About Guns Being Walked to Mexican Drug Cartels," *Desert Morning News*, October 4, 2011.

[159] Sharyl Attkisson, "ATF Investigation Expands to White House Staffers," *CBS News*, September 9, 2011.

[160] Letter from Representative Lamar Smith, Chairman of the House Committee on the Judiciary, to Attorney General Eric H. Holder, Jr., regarding interviews with senior Department of Justice staff about Operation Fast and Furious, January 31, 2012, http://judiciary.house.gov/news/pdfs/01312012%20Letter%20to%20ATG.pdf.

[161] U.S. Congress, *Fatally Flawed: Five Years of Gunwalking in Arizona*, U.S. House of Representatives, Committee on Oversight and Government Reform, Minority Staff Report, 112th Cong., 2nd Sess., January 2012, (continued...)

---

to Wide Receiver (2006-2007), this report describes two other Phoenix-based ATF investigations that involved gun walking: Hernandez (2007) and Medrano (2008). Representative Cummings also argued that former Attorney General Michael Mukasey ought to be called before the committee to testify, because the gun-walking tactics had originated during the Administration of President George W. Bush.

Also of note, during the hearing, Representative Gerald Connolly questioned Attorney General Holder about the need for tougher gun laws. The Attorney General responded that the Obama Administration had consistently favored reinstituting the semiautomatic assault weapons ban. Representative Connolly remarked that there had been no congressional hearing held so far on that topic or any other gun control proposal, yet the Attorney General had been questioned about Operation Fast and Furious on at least six previous occasions before various congressional committees. Chairman Issa countered that some of those hearings were appropriations hearings, at which Operation Fast and Furious was not the predominant issue. He also noted that, to date, the Obama Administration had not submitted any gun control-related legislative proposals to Congress. In turn, Representative Connolly asked the Attorney General if that were so. While the Attorney General did not comment upon any Administration-requested legislative proposals, he replied that he would be happy to submit a proposal to Congress for consideration and added that he thought that an anti-gun trafficking bill (H.R. 2554) introduced by Representative Carolyn Maloney would make a good starting point.

On February 14, 2012, Chairman Issa sent the Attorney General a followup letter, in which he conveyed the committee's increasing frustration with the department. He questioned, among other things, why Patrick Cunningham, the former Criminal Chief of the U.S. Attorney's Office in Arizona, asserted his Fifth Amendment privilege against self-incrimination rather than testify before the committee. Regarding outstanding committee requests for documents and other information related to the operation, Representative Issa emphasized that the committee's subpoena is not optional, and that a failure to produce the requested documents was a violation of federal law. He went on to write that "By any measure, the Department has obstructed and slowed our [the committee's] work."[162]

On May 3, 2012, Representative Issa, Chairman of the Committee on Oversight and Government Reform, released a staff briefing paper and draft resolution to cite Attorney General Holder in contempt of Congress for not complying with subpoenas issued by the committee for DOJ documents related to Operation Fast and Furious. The staff briefing paper includes the following statement, alleging that "For over a year, the Department has issued false denials, given answers intended to misdirect investigators, sought to intimidate witnesses, unlawfully withheld subpoenaed documents, and waited to be confronted with indisputable evidence before acknowledging uncomfortable facts."[163]

(...continued)

http://www.scribd.com/doc/79930290/%E2%80%9CFatally-Flawed-Five-Years-of-Gunwalking-in-Arizona-%E2%80%9D?tw_p=twt .

[162] Letter from Representative Darrell Issa, Chairman of the House Committee on Oversight and Government Reform, to Attorney General Eric H. Holder, Jr., regarding an October 12, 2011, subpoena for Operation Fast and Furious-related documents and a February 1, 2012, departmental request for a deadline extension for those documents, February 14, 2012, http://oversight.house.gov/images/stories/Letters/2012-02-14_DEI_to_Holder-DOJ_-_Contempt.pdf.

[163] Memorandum from Representative Darrell Issa, Chairman of the House Committee on Oversight and Government Reform, to Members of the Committee, regarding an "Update on Operation Fast and Furious," May 3, 2012, p. 10. For a copy of this staff briefing paper and draft resolution report, go to http://oversight.house.gov/wp-content/uploads/2012/ (continued...)

On May 10, 2012, during House consideration of the FY2013 CJS Appropriations bill (H.R. 5326), two amendments were passed that also addressed Operation Fast and Furious. Representative Trey Gowdy offered an amendment (H.Amdt. 1049) that reduced the DOJ General Administration account by $1.0 million and applied it to the spending reduction account. Representative Gowdy expressed his dissatisfaction with DOJ officials who have not complied with a committee subpoenas for greater information about Operation Fast and Furious. The Gowdy amendment passed by voice vote. Representatives Jason Chaffetz, Paul Gosar, and Blake Farenthold offered an amendment (H.Amdt. 1068) that would prohibit the expenditure of any funding provided under the bill in contravention to a criminal provision related to fraud and false statements (18 U.S.C. §1001(a)). This amendment was passed on a recorded vote: 381-41 (Roll no. 226).

ATF Firearms Tracing for Mexican Authorities

Although the United States does not maintain a registry of firearms or firearm owners (except for machineguns and destructive devices), as described above, ATF and federally licensed gun dealers maintain a decentralized system of transaction records, through which ATF can sometimes trace a firearm from its manufacturer or importer to its first private owner of record.[164] Over the years, successful firearm traces have generated leads in criminal investigations and have generated data that illustrate wider trafficking trends and patterns.

To support Project Gunrunner, ATF developed and deployed a Spanish-language version of its eTrace program for Mexican authorities to submit trace requests electronically to the United States. However, it should be underscored that not all firearms seized by Mexican authorities are traced, and trace submissions are more likely to be made for firearms believed to have originated in the United States. Moreover, problems persist with regard to the quality, quantity, and timeliness of firearms trace requests made by Mexican authorities and resultant data.[165] Data on some firearms, for example, were submitted several times. If previous tracing trends hold true, moreover, about a quarter of trace requests would have failed because the firearm make, model, or serial number was erroneously entered into the system.[166] It is also probable that ATF was only

---

(...continued)

05/Update-on-Fast-and-Furious-with-attachment-FINAL.pdf.

For further information on congressional subpoenas and contempt citations, see CRS Report RL34097, *Congress's Contempt Power and the Enforcement of Congressional Subpoenas: Law, History, Practice, and Procedure*, by Todd Garvey and Alissa M. Dolan.

[164] The key identifying element associated with each firearm and its related record of manufacture, importation, or transfer is the firearm's serial number. Through the firearm's serial number, ATF can identify the manufacturer or importer, contact them, and find out the wholesale or retail dealer to whom they transferred the firearm in question. In recent years, many firearms manufacturers and importers have given ATF electronic access to such records in order to respond to ATF trace requests more efficiently and expeditiously. By contacting the wholesale/retail dealer, ATF can then identify the first retail owner of record, assuming the dealer's recordkeeping is complete and the purchaser of the firearm did not misrepresent himself by adopting a false identity. However, while the GCA requires licensed gun dealers to maintain records on both new and secondhand firearm transfers, the linkage between the manufacturer/importer records and the wholesale/retail dealer records is broken after the first retail sale, because there is no mechanism under current law, through which ATF is informed when a secondhand firearm reenters the public course of commerce by being transferred from a private person back to a licensed gun dealer.

[165] Colby Goodman, *Update on U.S. Firearms Trafficking to Mexico Report*, Woodrow Wilson International Center for Scholars, Mexico Institute, April 2011, http://www.wilsoncenter.org/news/docs/Goodman%20Update%20on%20US%20Firearms%20to%20Mexico.pdf.

[166] Ibid.

---

able to identify the first private firearm owner of record or other possible sources in the United States in about a quarter of trace requests.

Nonetheless, trace data have proved to be a useful indicator of trafficking trends with regard to the types of firearms being trafficked, their possible sources, and how recently trafficked firearms were diverted from legal to illegal channels of commerce. Along these lines, GAO recommended that the Attorney General should direct ATF to regularly update its reporting on aggregate firearms trace data and trends in its June 2009 Project Gunrunner report. GAO also reported that ATF had traced more than 23,159 firearms from FY2004 through FY2008 for Mexican authorities.[167] Approximately 86.6% of those firearms were determined to have originated in the United States.[168] For the last three years (FY2006 through FY2008) of that study period, over 90% of firearms recovered in Mexico and traced by ATF were found to have originated in the United States.[169] Of those firearms, 68% were manufactured in the United States and 19% were manufactured abroad and imported into the United States.[170] About 70% of traced firearms were found to have come from Texas (39%), California (20%), and Arizona (10%). It is notable, however, that Mexican authorities had submitted only a fraction of the firearms that had been recovered in Mexico. In FY2008, for example, information on only about 7,200 of the nearly 30,000 firearms recovered by the Mexican Attorney General's office was submitted to ATF for tracing.[171]

In May 2010, Mexican President Felipe Calderon addressed a joint session of Congress and revealed that Mexican authorities had seized 75,000 firearms, of which 80% had been traced back to the United States.[172] According to ATF, this higher than previously reported number of traces reflected a batch submission of trace requests made by the Mexican Attorney General that changed the trace totals for previous years, which are reported by year of recovery.

In April 2011, the U.S. Embassy in Mexico City reported that ATF processed 78,194 trace requests for Mexican authorities from FY2007 through FY2010.[173] Based on previous trace data, a large percentage of these trace requests would have involved firearms that were either manufactured in or imported into the United States for civilian markets, but such a percentage was not released by the Embassy.[174] However, a significantly smaller percentage would have been successfully traced to the first private owner of record. Noticeably absent were any data on firearms with a short "time-to-recovery,"[175] that is, the time interval between the initial retail sale

---

[167] U.S. Government Accountability Office, *Firearms Trafficking: U.S. Efforts to Combat Arms Trafficking to Mexico Face Planning and Coordination Challenges*, GAO-09-709, June 2009, p. 18.

[168] Ibid., p. 15.

[169] Ibid.

[170] Ibid., p. 16.

[171] Ibid.

[172] Mary Beth Sheridan, "Mexico's Calderon Tells Congress He Needs U.S. Help in Fighting Drug Wars," *Washington Post*, May 21, 2010, p. A02.

[173] U.S. Embassy in Mexico City, "Fact Sheet: Combating Arms Trafficking," April 2011.

[174] U.S. Government Accountability Office, *Firearms Trafficking: U.S. Efforts to Combat Arms Trafficking to Mexico Face Planning and Coordination Challenges*, GAO-09-709, June 2009, pp. 5-6.

[175] ATF employed the term "time-to-crime." Some view "time-to-crime" to be a misnomer, because some traced firearms may not have been directly linked to a crime. Furthermore, their time-of-recovery by law enforcement may not reflect precisely when, if ever, traced firearms were used in a crime. In addition, traced firearms might have been legally imported into Mexico for civilian or military purposes. It is unknown whether ATF has access to U.S. export data that would allow for the exclusion of such firearms from their trace accounts. Nevertheless, "time-to-recovery" (continued...)

---

of a firearm by a federally licensed gun dealer to a private person and the firearm's recovery by law enforcement. A short time-to-recovery is one possible indicator that the firearm had been trafficked or stolen. Nor did the Embassy press release include any data on type, make, model, and caliber of the most frequently traced firearms. For trend analysis, such data would have been useful for total firearms traced, as well as for different time periods.[176]

In June 2011, ATF released limited trace data to the Senate Caucus on International Narcotics Control.[177] The Senate Caucus reported that ATF processed 29,284 trace requests on firearms that were recovered by Mexican authorities in calendar years 2009 and 2010. Of those firearms, 20,504 (70%) were either manufactured in or imported into the United States. ATF did not provide any data on successful traces that resulted in identifying the first private owner of record, the time-to-recovery of traced firearms, or the most frequently traced firearms by type, make, model, and caliber. These omissions, in part, prompted Senator Grassley to write then ATF Acting Director Kenneth Melson with "questions about why ATF provided some select information, but not a more detailed analysis that would help Congress, and the American people, better understand the causes and sources of illegal firearms in Mexico."[178] Senator Grassley expressed his concern that press accounts that focused exclusively on U.S. manufactured or imported firearms as a percentage of total trace requests submitted by Mexican authorities were misleading.[179] Senator Grassley also cited an article that reported that a significant quantity of firearms that had been recovered by or turned over to the Mexican Army, as opposed to the Mexican Attorney General, had not been submitted to ATF for tracing.[180]

With the limited release of trace data, it became and probably remains less clear whether the flow of illegal guns consists of an "ant run" that has trickled across the border over the decades as individuals or small, independent organizations have smuggled firearms into Mexico for a variety of purposes, or an "iron river of guns" that has surged in recent years as Mexican DTOs have sought to arm themselves with firearms that are commonly available on the U.S. civilian market. When available, trace data suggest that the majority of firearms submitted for tracing originated in the United States, given that these firearms were either embossed with a U.S. manufacturer or importer's stamp. However, it is probable that a much smaller percentage of these firearms were successfully traced to the first U.S. private owner of record. More importantly, several substantive methodological limitations preclude using trace data as a proxy for the larger population of crime guns in Mexico or the United States. While the United States could be the largest source of crime

---

(...continued)

gives policy makers a rough time interval, during which traced firearms were possibly stolen or trafficked.

[176] In several conversations with ATF officials, the author was told that the agency was reluctant to release data on the make of firearms, because the press and interest groups had focused on the firearm manufacturers as being corrupt causing a public relations problem, because the manufacturers were engaged in lawful activities with regards to making and selling of these firearms.

[177] ATF released limited trace data to the Senate Caucus on International Narcotics Control in June 2011. See U.S. Senate Caucus on International Narcotics Control, *Halting U.S. Firearms Trafficking to Mexico: A Report by Senators Dianne Feinstein, Charles Schumer, and Sheldon Whitehouse*, 112th Cong., 1st sess., June 2011, p. 6.

[178] Letter from Senator Charles E. Grassley to Acting ATF Director Kenneth Melson, regarding the selective release of firearms trace data, June 16, 2011, http://grassley.senate.gov/judiciary/upload/Guns-06-16-11-signed-letter-to-Melson-incomplete-gun-data.pdf.

[179] Ibid.

[180] For example, Senator Grassley cited a news report in which it was reported that, in May 2009, the Mexican Army held over 305,424 recovered weapons, the bulk of which had not been traced by ATF. See E. Eduardo Castillo, "AP IMPACT: Mexico's Weapons Cache Stymies Tracing," *Associated Press Online*, May 7, 2009.

---

guns in Mexico, trace data do not conclusively establish that assertion as fact. In addition, another consideration could be the possibility that the 78,000 firearms that were submitted by Mexico's Attorney General for tracing represent a proverbial "pig in the python." Unknown, but possibly significant, percentages of these firearms could have been illegally smuggled into Mexico over decades. Moreover, while there is little evidence to suggest that Mexican DTOs are acquiring military grade firearms directly from sources within the United States, these organizations are arguably capable of acquiring such firearms and other military armaments (e.g., recoilless rifles, rocket launchers, and grenades) from other illicit, international sources given the profitability of the illegal drug trade.

In the Consolidated and Further Continuing Appropriations Act, 2012 (P.L. 112-55; H.R. 2112), conferees included report language (H.Rept. 112-284, p. 240) that requires ATF to provide the Committees on Appropriations with annual data on the total number of firearms recovered by the Government of Mexico, and of those, the number for which an ATF trace is attempted, the number successfully traced and the number determined to be manufactured in or imported into the United States prior to being recovered in Mexico.

On April 26, 2012, in compliance with the provision described above, ATF released revised but limited trace data for calendar years 2007 through 2011. ATF underscored that the Government of Mexico did not and does not provide it with data on the total number of firearms seized in that country, nor did the agency make any attempt to estimate the number of firearms seized in that country. Nevertheless, of 99,691 firearms submitted by Mexican authorities to ATF for tracing for those calendar years (2007-2011), 68,161 (68.3%) were considered to be U.S.-sourced, in that those firearms were either originally manufactured in or imported into the United States. Of those U.S.-sourced firearms, 27,825 (27.9%) were traced back to the initial purchaser, or the first retail purchaser of record. And, another 1,461 (1.4%) of those U.S.-sourced firearms were legitimately exported to Mexico from a U.S. gun dealer to a Mexican law enforcement or government agency. While ATF did not provide any data on the make, model, or caliber of (1) U.S.-sourced firearms, (2) firearms traced back to the initial purchaser, or (3) traced firearms with a short time-to-recovery, it did provide breakdowns by type of firearm. ATF noted that the percentage of firearms submitted for tracing that were rifles had shifted markedly during those years. For example, for 2007 rifles accounted for 28.2% of firearms submitted for tracing. That percentage increased to 58.6% for 2010 and decreased somewhat to 43.3% for 2011.[181]

Veterans, Mental Incompetency, and Firearms Eligibility

The 112th Congress has revisited the issue of veterans, mental incompetency, and firearms eligibility. On July 22, 2011, the House Committee on Veterans' Affairs Subcommittee on Disability and Memorials marked up and reported a veterans' benefits bill (H.R. 2349). During markup, Representative Denny Rehberg successfully offered an amendment to the bill that would prohibit the Department of Veterans Affairs (VA) from determining a beneficiary to be mentally incompetent for the purposes of gun control, unless such a determination were made by a judge, magistrate, or other judicial authority based upon a finding that the beneficiary posed a danger to himself or others. As described below, similar amendments were considered in the 110th and 111th Congresses. On October 6, 2011, the full committee approved this bill. On October 11, 2011, the

---

[181] For more information, ATF has posted trace data for Mexico, Canada, and the Caribbean on its website, http://www.atf.gov/statistics/.

House passed H.R. 2349 by a voice vote. It includes the Rehberg amendment, which reflects a bill (H.R. 1898) that Representative Rehberg previously introduced on May 13, 2011. Senator Burr introduced a similar bill (S. 1707) on October 13, 2011.

Proponents of the Veterans Second Amendment Protection Act, like the NRA, view the current VA policy as placing an unwarranted indignity on men and women, in many cases at the end of their lives, who have previously served their country honorably in the Armed Forces. Arguably, some of those veterans referred by the VA to the FBI as having been "adjudicated as mental defective" may have only been mentally incapacitated due to age or other related infirmities, as opposed to suffering from a severe mental illness or disability that caused them to behave in a threatening or dangerous manner. Opponents of the proposal, like the Brady Campaign, have countered that the VA has demonstrated due diligence by complying with the law and, by doing so, has increased public safety. They could argue further that the VA's current policy does not diminish national recognition of those veterans' honorable service; instead, it has been implemented to protect those veterans and others from the harm that might occur if they acquired a firearm and used it improperly. For a fuller discussion of underlying issues, see **Appendix A**.

ATF FY2012 and FY2013 Appropriations

The ATF enforces federal criminal law related to the manufacture, importation, and distribution of alcohol, tobacco, firearms, and explosives. ATF works independently and through partnerships with industry groups; international, state and local governments; and other federal agencies to investigate and reduce crime involving firearms and explosives, acts of arson, and illegal trafficking of alcohol and tobacco products.

Figure 1. ATF Appropriations, FY2001-FY2012

(dollars in millions)

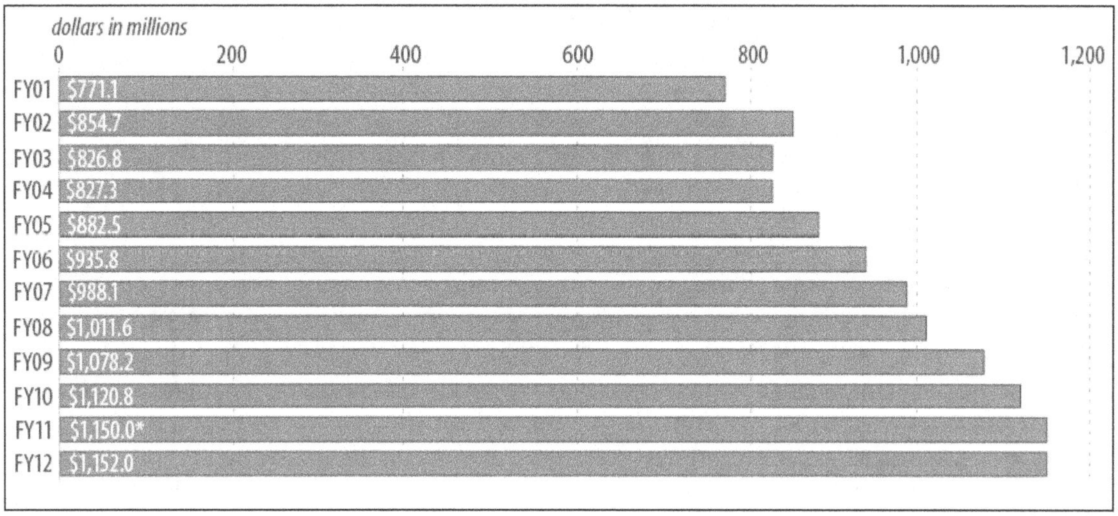

Source: Department of the Treasury and Department of Justice congressional budget submissions.

Notes: *The FY2011 appropriation includes $37.5 million that was provided to ATF under the FY2010/FY2011 Southwest border supplemental appropriation (P.L. 111-230), because most of that funding was obligated for FY2011.

Congress usually funds ATF in the Commerce-Justice-Science (CJS) appropriations bill. In the absence of an enacted bill for FY2012, Congress passed a continuing resolution (P.L. 112-36) that funded ATF at its FY2011 level (less 1.503%) through November 18, 2011.[182] As discussed further below, Congress passed full-year CJS appropriations in the Consolidated and Further Continuing Appropriations Act, 2012 (H.R. 2112; H.Rept. 112-284), which the President signed into law (P.L. 112-55) on November 18, 2011. For FY2012, this act provided ATF with $1.152 billion, or nearly $39.5 million more than the previous year. In part, the increased appropriation for FY2012 reflects that the FY2010/FY2011 Southwest border supplemental appropriation was annualized in that year's appropriation. As reflected in **Figure 1**, if the $37.5 million FY2010/FY2011 Southwest border supplemental were included in ATF's FY2011 appropriation, the FY2012 appropriation would reflect a considerably smaller increase, $2.0 million.

FY2013 Request

For FY2013, the Administration has requested $1.153 billion for ATF. Although this amount reflects a net increase of about $1.3 million, the FY2013 request includes no new budget enhancements for ATF. Instead, it anticipates over $26.9 million in savings or other offsets in either contract reductions ($24.8 million) or information technology savings ($2.1 million). As **Figure 2** shows, the largest portion ($875.5 million, or 76%) of the requested appropriation would be allocated to the firearms budget decision unit. The second-largest portion ($253.7 million, or 22%) would be allocated to the arson and explosives budget decision unit. The remainder ($23.1 million, or 2%) would be

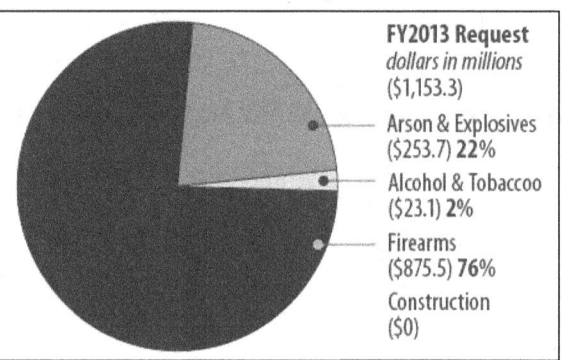

Figure 2. ATF Appropriations, FY2013 Request

FY2013 Request
dollars in millions
($1,153.3)

Arson & Explosives ($253.7) **22%**
Alcohol & Tobaccoo ($23.1) **2%**
Firearms ($875.5) **76%**
Construction ($0)

Source: ATF Congressional Budget Submission, FY2013.

allocated to the alcohol and tobacco diversion budget decision unit. By percentage, these allocations are comparable to those reported by ATF to correspond with the agency's FY2012 enacted appropriation.

Also of significance, the Administration's request includes proposals to strip out futurity language that was attached to two ATF appropriations riders during the FY2012 appropriations cycle making those riders permanent law. The first rider prohibits ATF from consolidating or centralizing within DOJ the records of firearms acquisitions and dispositions (or any portion thereof) that federally licensed gun dealers are required by law to maintain. When gun dealers go out of business, however, those records are forwarded to ATF. And, the second rider prohibits ATF from electronically searching those out-of-business records by name or any personal identification code. For evidentiary purposes, those records are maintained on microform. For retrieval and storage purposes, out-of-business records are maintained in a digital format, so those records may be searched electronically by firearm serial number, but not by owner (first retail buyer of record). In addition, the Administration's request would strip out futurity language (inserted for FY2008 and every year thereafter) included in a controversial ATF appropriations rider known as the Tiahrt amendment. For a fuller discussion of underlying issues, see **Appendix A**.

---

[182] For further information, see CRS Report RL30343, *Continuing Resolutions: Latest Action and Brief Overview of Recent Practices*, by Sandy Streeter.

On April 19, 2012, the Senate Committee on Appropriations reported an FY2013 funding measure (S. 2323) that would provide ATF with the same amount as requested by the Administration ($1.153 billion). The Senate bill, however, does not follow the Administration's request to strip the futurity language out of ATF appropriations riders that were made permanent in the previous year's appropriations act (P.L. 112-55). On the one hand, Senate report language (S.Rept. 112-158, p. 73) noted that Operation Fast and Furious was only one part of ATF's Southwest border operations to reduce illegal gun trafficking to Mexico. On the other hand, language was included in the departmental general provisions that would continue to prohibit the expenditure of any funding under the bill from being used to facilitate the transfer of an operable firearm to a known or suspected agent of a drug cartel (§217). Another provision would continue to prohibit ATF from issuing regulations that would prohibit the importation of certain types of shotguns (§538). Yet another provision, which may have implications for ATF, prohibits any U.S. Attorney from holding multiple jobs outside of the scope of a U.S. Attorney's professional duty (§213). As described above, the U.S. Attorney for the District of Minnesota, B. Todd Jones, is currently serving as the interim acting ATF Director.

On April 26, 2012, the House Committee on Appropriations approved a similar FY2013 funding measure (H.R. 5326) that would also provide the same amount for ATF ($1.153 billion). This measure also includes provisions that are similar to those included in the Senate-reported bill described above (§§217, 536, and 213). In addition, the House measure includes futurity language in three additional long-standing prohibitions (riders) included in the ATF salaries and expenses appropriations language. These provisions would prohibit ATF from

- altering the regulatory definition of "curios and relics,"[183]

- requiring federally licensed gun dealers to conduct physical inventories,"[184] or

- revoking a federal firearms license for lack of business activity.

In addition, during House full committee markup, Representative Rehberg successfully offered an amendment that would prohibit ATF from requiring multiple long gun sales reports. As described below, a similar Rehberg-sponsored amendment was included in the FY2012 House bill, but it was not included in an enacted bill. On May 10, 2012, the House passed H.R. 5326, amended. Two amendments reduced ATF funding for FY2013 to $1.151 billion, or $537,000 less than the FY2012 appropriation.[185]

---

[183] See 27 CFR §478.11 for the definition of "curios and relics," which generally include firearms that are 50 years old, of museum interest, or derive a substantial amount of their value from the fact that they are novel, rare, bizarre, or because they are associated with some historical figure, period, or event. For a list of "curios and relics," go to http://www.atf.gov/firearms/curios/index htm. Federally licensed firearms collectors are authorized to engage in limited interstate transfers of "curios and relics," whereas in nearly all cases an unlicensed person must engage the services of a federally licensed gun dealer to facilitate interstate firearms transfers to another unlicensed person.

[184] This provision was also originally part of the Tiahrt amendment.

[185] During House floor consideration, however, Representative Colleen Hanabusa offered an amendment (H.Amdt. 1046) to reduce the ATF appropriation by $1.9 million and increase the NOAA appropriation (described above) by $1.6 million. In addition, the House considered another amendment (H.Amdt. 1090) to reduce the ATF appropriation by $18,000. The House approved both amendments by voice votes.

FY2012 Request and Appropriation

For FY2012, the Administration requested $1.147 billion for ATF.[186] This amount would have funded 5,147 FTE positions and 5,181 permanent positions. Although it would have provided a $34.8 million increase (3.1%) over ATF's enacted FY2011 appropriation, nearly all of this increase would have been for increases to the agency's base budget, including the annualized $37.5 million Southwest border supplemental appropriation.[187] Correspondingly, the Administration anticipated offsets and savings of $27.3 million, as well as a program increase of $1.5 million as a budget enhancement for ATF to participate in a DOJ-wide initiative to increase law enforcement electronic surveillance capabilities nationally. Reductions included $10.0 million in the National Integrated Ballistic Information Network (NIBIN), $4.0 million in reduced training opportunities for state and local law enforcement, and $1.0 in the alcohol and tobacco program. According to the ATF, the remaining $12.3 million in reductions that would be sustained through other administrative efficiencies and cost reductions. As noted above and described below, Congress appropriated ATF $1.152 billion for FY2012.

Figure 3. ATF Appropriations: FY2012 Requested and Enacted Compared

(dollars in millions)

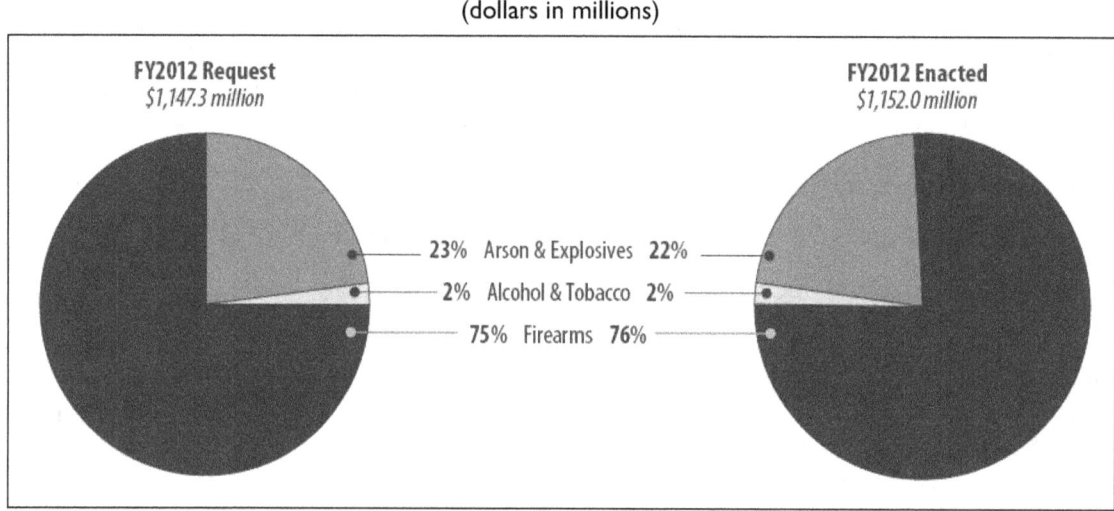

Source: ATF Congressional Budget Submissions, Fiscal Years 2012 and 2013.

Figure 3 shows budget decision unit allocations, as proposed in the FY2012 budget request and as reported in the FY2013 budget request. Under the request, the firearms compliance and investigations decision unit was to be allocated the lion's share, 75%, of appropriated funding. Under the enacted appropriation, it was allocated 76%. The arson and explosives investigations

---

[186] U.S. Department of Justice, Bureau of Alcohol, Tobacco, Firearms and Explosives, *Congressional Budget Submission, Fiscal Year 2012*, February 2011, http://www.justice.gov/jmd/2012justification/pdf/fy12-atf-justification.pdf.

[187] Congress finalized ATF's FY2011 appropriation in the Department of Defense and Full-Year Continuing Appropriations Act, 2011 (H.R. 1473; P.L. 112-10). Under this act, Congress provided $1.113 billion for ATF for FY2011, or $8.2 million less than the previous year's appropriation. It is significant to note that neither amount, the $1.121 billion for FY2010 or the $1.113 billion for FY2011, reflect an FY2010/FY2011 Southwest border supplemental of $37.5 million, which was provided at the end of FY2010. Because of the timing of the supplemental, for accounting purposes it arguably could be added to either fiscal year. However, it was largely obligated in FY2011. Added to that year's appropriation, ATF's FY2011 appropriation increases to about $1.150 billion. And, instead of an $8.2 million reduction, ATF had an additional $29.3 million in budget authority for FY2011.

decision unit and the alcohol and tobacco diversion decision unit were to be allocated 23% and 2%, respectively, of the requested appropriation. Under the enacted appropriation, however, the arson and explosives investigations decision unit was allocated 22%.

On July 20, 2011, the House Committee reported an FY2012 CJS appropriations bill (H.R. 2596; H.Rept. 112-169). This measure would have provided ATF with $1.111 billion, $1.1 million (0.1%) less than the FY2011 enacted amount and $35.9 million (3.1%) less than the Administration's FY2012 request.[188] In full committee markup, the bill was amended with two firearms-related amendments. One, described above, would have prohibited ATF from implementing an OMB-approved information collection initiative, under which federally licensed gun dealers in Southwest border states are required to submit multiple sales reports for certain semiautomatic rifles to ATF. As discussed below, this provision was not included in the enacted FY2012 appropriation. The other would prohibit ATF from implementing additional restrictions on the importation of certain shotguns that include certain features (e.g., pistol grips, folding or collapsible stocks, laser sights, and the ability to accept large capacity ammunition feeding devices) that ATF has determined to be non-sporting.[189] This prohibition was included in the enacted FY2012 appropriation. Moreover, H.R. 2596 included language of "futurity" in several firearms-related riders. As described below, similar language was included in three provisions in the enacted appropriation.

On September 15, 2011, the Senate Committee on Appropriations reported an FY2012 CJS appropriations bill (S. 1572; S.Rept. 112-78) that would have provided $1.09 billion for ATF, $22.3 million (2.0%) less than the FY2011-enacted amount, $57 million (5.0%) less than the Administration's request of $1.147 billion, and $21.1 million (1.9%) less than the House mark. The Senate folded S. 1572 into a Minibus appropriations bill (H.R. 2112) and passed this measure. In addition to the Senate-passed Cornyn amendment (S.Amdt. 775, discussed above), several other firearms-related amendments were offered but not voted upon. For example, Senators Mark Begich and Orrin Hatch offered an amendment to broaden the circumstances under which handguns could be transferred legally in interstate commerce (S.Amdt. 786). Senator Dean Heller offered an amendment to prohibit ATF from implementing its Southwest border multiple rifle sales reporting requirement (S.Amdt. 843). Similar language, as described above, has been included in the House-reported bill (H.R. 2596). Senator Hatch also offered three amendments to include language of "futurity" into firearms-related riders accompanying the ATF appropriation (S.Amdt. 745, S.Amdt. 770, and S.Amdt. 875). The House-reported and -passed bill included similar futurity language. Senator Jon Tester offered an amendment that would overturn an ATF ruling that persons who have medical marijuana prescriptions are ineligible to possess a firearms (S.Amdt. 882).

On November 14, 2011, House and Senate conferees reported H.R. 2112 (H.Rept. 112-284), which has been enacted (P.L. 112-55). It provides ATF with $1.152 billion for FY2012. This amount is $39.5 million (3.5%) greater than the FY2011 enacted amount, $4.7 million (0.4%) greater that the FY2012 request, $40.6 million (3.7%) greater than the House-reported amount, and $61.7 million (5.7%) greater than Senate-passed amount. As discussed above, this act

---

[188] During full committee markup, Representative Sam Farr successfully offered an amendment that cut discretionary accounts in the bill by 0.1%, and shifted that funding ($48 million) to the National Oceanic and Atmospheric Administration's Operations, Research, and Facilities program.

[189] U.S. Department of Justice, Bureau of Alcohol, Tobacco, Firearms and Explosives, Firearms and Explosives Industry Division, *ATF Study on the Importability of Certain Shotguns*, January 2011, http://www.atf.gov/firearms/industry/january-2011-importability-of-certain-shotguns.pdf.

includes revised language that reflects the Cornyn amendment. This provision (§219) prohibits any federal law enforcement officer from facilitating the delivery of an operable firearm to an individual known or suspected of being connected to a drug cartel. It also includes "futurity" language that makes three long-standing annual appropriations riders permanent law. For FY2012 and every year thereafter, these riders prohibit

- DOJ from consolidating or centralizing any records maintained by federally licensed gun dealers related to the acquisition and disposition of firearms;[190]

- ATF from electronically retrieving firearm transfer records that have been submitted to ATF, when federally licensed gun dealers go out business, by searching those out-of-business records by any individual's name or other personal identification code;[191] and

- the FBI from charging a fee in connection with a Brady background checks for firearms transfer and possession eligibility, and requires further that the FBI destroy all Brady background check records related to approved firearm transfer records within 24 hours (§511).

In addition, the act includes a provision (§541) that is similar to House language that would prevent ATF from implementing additional restrictions on the importation of certain shotguns, as well as report language requiring ATF to report to the House and Senate Appropriations Committees annually on firearm trace requests processed for Mexican authorities.

FISA Sunset Extensions and Firearms-Related Amendments[192]

On May 12, 2011, the House Judiciary Committee considered a bill, the FISA Sunsets Reauthorization Act of 2011 (H.R. 1800), to extend certain expiring provisions of the Foreign Intelligence Surveillance Act (FISA).[193] In full committee markup, Representative Mike Quigley offered an amendment that would have allowed the Attorney General to deny a firearms transfer to any person about whom the Attorney General gathered information during the course of a national security investigation (under FISA), if that information generated a "reasonable belief" that the firearm(s) might be used by the prospective transferee in terrorism-related conduct.[194] This amendment was defeated by a vote of 11 to 21.[195]

During Senate consideration of similar bill, the PATRIOT Sunsets Extension Act of 2011 (S. 1038 and S. 990), Senator Rand Paul offered several versions of an amendment (S.Amdt. 328, S.Amdt. 363, and S.Amdt. 373) that would have exempted certain "firearms records" from the business records that can be secretly obtained by FBI agents during a FISA national security investigation

---

[190] Proviso in ATF salaries and expenses language.

[191] Ibid.

[192] For information on FISA provisions that were due to sunset, see CRS Report R40138, *Amendments to the Foreign Intelligence Surveillance Act (FISA) Extended Until June 1, 2015*, by Edward C. Liu.

[193] 50 U.S.C. §1801 et al.

[194] To effect such a firearms transfer denial, the subject of the FISA investigation would most likely be placed on a NICS-accessible terrorist watch list (NCIC-KST). For further information, see the heading below, Brady Background and Terrorist Watch List Checks.

[195] U.S. Congress, House Committee on the Judiciary, *FISA Sunsets Reauthorization Act of 2011*, to accompany H.R. 1800, 112th Cong., 1st sess., May 18, 2011, p. 9.

(§215 of the USA PATRIOT Act, as amended[196]). On May 26, 2011, during consideration of S. 990, the Senate tabled S.Amdt. 363 by a vote of 85 to 10. Therefore, the amendment was not included in the enacted legislation (P.L. 112-14).

Tucson Shootings

Following the Tucson shootings, issues were raised about the shooter's mental illness and drug use, as well as his use of large capacity ammunition feeding devices (LCAFDs). Another issue that was raised was banning firearms within the proximity of certain high-level federal officials.

Mental Illness and Drug Use as Prohibiting Factors

As described above, persons who have been "adjudicated mental defective"[197] or who are "unlawful users of or addicted to any controlled substance"[198] are prohibited from possessing a firearm or having one transferred to them. The FBI maintains files on those persons as part of the NICS Index. According to the FBI, as of December 31, 2010, the NICS Index included 1,107,758 records on individuals who had been adjudicated mental defective.[199] Although the NICS Index included 2,092 records on individuals who are known to be drug users and addicts,[200] arrest records for drug offenses are also contained in the Interstate Identification Index (III).

Following the Virginia Tech mass shooting on April 16, 2007, Congress passed the NICS Improvement Amendments Act of 2007 (NIAA; P.L. 110-180), a law that established incentives to prompt state, local, and tribal governments to transfer mental defective files to the FBI for inclusion in the NICS Index. Although this act focused on mentally ill persons who were adjudicated to be a threat to themselves or others, it did not focus on drug users. As a consequence, Congress could revisit the NIAA to increase incentives for state, local, and tribal governments to transfer records on both categories of prohibited persons. Along these lines, Mayors Against Illegal Guns (MAIG) released a "plan to prevent further tragedies" like Tucson. The MAIG plan calls for the following steps:

---

[196] P.L. 107-56; October 26, 2001; 115 Stat. 287, codified at 50 U.SC. §1861. Section 215 requires the Foreign Intelligence Surveillance Court to approve all requests for such documents.

[197] For a definition of "adjudicated mental defective," see the "Mental Defective Adjudications" section on p. 38.

[198] Under 27 C.F.R. §478.11, an "unlawful user of or addicted to any controlled substance" means a person who uses a controlled substance and has lost the power of self-control with reference to the use of [a] controlled substance; and any person who is a current user of a controlled substance in a manner other than as prescribed by a licensed physician. Such use is not limited to the use of drugs on a particular day, or within a matter of days or weeks before, but rather that the unlawful use has occurred recently enough to indicate that the individual is actively engaged in such conduct. A person may be an unlawful current user of a controlled substance even though the substance is not being used at the precise time the person seeks to acquire a firearm or receives or possesses a firearm. An inference of current use may be drawn from evidence of a recent use or possession of a controlled substance or a pattern of use or possession that reasonably covers the present time, e.g., a conviction for use or possession of a controlled substance within the past year; multiple arrests for such offenses within the past five years if the most recent arrest occurred within the past year; or persons found through a drug test to use a controlled substance unlawfully, provided that the test was administered within the past year. For a current or former member of the Armed Forces, an inference of current use may be drawn from recent disciplinary or other administrative action based on confirmed drug use, e.g., court-martial conviction, nonjudicial punishment, or an administrative discharge based on drug use or drug rehabilitation failure.

[199] See http://www.fbi.gov/about-us/cjis/nics/reports/nics-index.

[200] Ibid.

- fully funding the NICS Improvement Amendments Act (P.L. 110-180) to help agencies and states cover the costs of gathering records on prohibited persons and making them electronically available to the FBI;

- providing larger cuts (up to 50%) to a wider array of federal law enforcement assistance grant programs[201] for not providing such records than what is currently provided for under P.L. 110-180;

- requiring every federal agency to certify to the Attorney General twice a year that all disqualifying records, including those related to drug use or addiction, have been electronically provided to the FBI;

- clarifying and expanding regulatory definitions related to mental health and drug use; and

- safeguarding the rights of people who are listed in databases queried by NICS.[202]

Senator Charles Schumer introduced a bill that would amend P.L. 110-180 to advance certain deadlines and apply deeper cuts to a wider array of federal law enforcement assistance grant programs (S. 436). Representative Carolyn McCarthy introduced an identical measure (H.R. 1781). Representatives McCarthy and John Dingell have reportedly submitted a request to GAO for an assessment of weaknesses in firearms-related background check procedures.[203] On November 15, 2011, the Senate Committee on the Judiciary's Subcommittee on Crime and Terrorism held a hearing on the Fix Gun Checks Act of 2011 (S. 436/H.R. 1781).

Large Capacity Ammunition Feeding Devices

The Tucson shooter was reportedly armed with a 9mm Glock 19 semiautomatic pistol loaded with 31 rounds in a 33-round extended magazine.[204] This pistol is normally equipped with a 15-round magazine, two of which the shooter also had on his person. He also had another 33-round extended magazine.[205] He managed to fire at least 31 shots, emptying a single magazine. He killed 6 people and wounded another 13, including Representative Giffords. Three bystanders, one of whom was wounded, managed to subdue the shooter as he attempted to reload his second 30-plus round magazine. Representative McCarthy has introduced a bill to reinstate a ban on magazines that are capable of accommodating more than 10 rounds (H.R. 308). Such a ban was in effect from September 13, 1994, through September 13, 2004, as part of the larger semiautomatic assault weapons ban (described below). Senator Frank Lautenberg has introduced a similar bill (S. 32).

---

[201] According to MAIG, such programs could include the State Criminal Alien Assistance Program, Title II Juvenile Justice Grants, Juvenile Accountability Block Grants, and Enforcing Underage Drinking Laws Block Grants.

[202] Mayors Against Illegal Guns, "A Plan to Prevent Future Tragedies," January 2011, http://www.mayorsagainstillegalguns.org.

[203] James V. Grimaldi and Sari Horwitz, "Cuts Threaten ATF's Efforts to Stem Flow of Guns South," *Washington Post*, January 31, 2011, p. 1.

[204] David A. Fahrenthold and Clarence Williams, "Congresswoman Shot in Tucson Rampage," *Washington Post*, January 9, 2011, p. A1.

[205] Most semiautomatic pistol magazines, or clips, are designed to be self-contained within the handle of the pistol. The 33 round extended magazines used by the shooter protrude well beneath the butt of the pistol handle.

Banning Firearms within the Proximity of Federal Officials

Representatives Laura Richardson and Peter King have introduced bills (H.R. 367 and H.R. 496) that would prohibit most people from carrying a firearm within 1,000 feet of certain high-level federal officials while those officials were holding a public event, campaigning for office, or otherwise acting in an official capacity. Both bills arguably are modeled on the Gun Free School Zone Act of 1990 (P.L. 101-647), which prohibits firearm possession in a school zone (on the campus of a public or private school or within 1,000 feet of the grounds).[206]

Other Salient Gun Control Legislative Issues

Other salient firearms-related issues that continue to receive attention include (1) screening firearms background check applicants against terrorist watch lists; (2) reforming the regulation of federally licensed gun dealers; (3) requiring background checks for private firearms transfers at gun shows; (4) more-strictly regulating certain firearms previously defined in statute as "semiautomatic assault weapons"; and (5) banning or requiring the registration of certain long-range .50 caliber rifles, which are commonly referred to as "sniper" rifles.

Terrorist Watch List Screening and Brady Background Checks[207]

On November 5, 2009, U.S. Army Major Nidal Malik Hasan shot 13 persons to death and wounded over 30 at Fort Hood, TX. Prior to the shootings, Hasan had corresponded by email with a radical Muslim imam, Anwar al-Aulaqi, who U.S. authorities had long suspected of having substantial ties to al-Qaeda.[208] Although FBI counterterrorism agents were aware of Hasan's communications with al-Aulaqi,[209] it was unclear at what level Hasan was being scrutinized by the FBI.[210] If he had been the subject of a full counterterrorism investigation, FBI policy would have required that he be watch-listed.[211] Depending upon the sequence of events, had Hasan been watch-listed, there is a possibility that his purchase of a pistol[212] and the required Brady background check could have alerted FBI counterterrorism agents to that transfer, and they might have been able to take steps that would have prevented the shootings. The Fort Hood shootings

---

[206] For the statutory definition of a "school zone," see 18 U.S.C. §921(a)(25). For the prohibition, see 18 U.S.C. §922(q).

[207] For further information, see CRS Report R42336, *Terrorist Watch List Screening and Brady Background Checks for Firearms*, by William J. Krouse.

[208] Carrie Johnson, Spencer C. Hsu, and Ellen Nakashima, "Hasan Had Intensified Contact with Cleric: FBI Monitored E-mail Exchanges Fort Hood Suspect Raised Prospect of Financial Transfers," *Washington Post*, November 21, 2009, p. A01.

[209] Philip Rucker, Carrie Johnson, and Ellen Nakashima, "Hasan E-mails to Cleric Didn't Result in Inquiry; Suspect in Fort Hood Shootings Will Be Tried in Military Court," *Washington Post*, November 10, 2009, p. A01.

[210] According to a November 11, 2009, FBI press release, Hasan's communications with Anwar al-Aulaqi were assessed by the FBI in connection with an investigation of another subject, and the content of those communications was explainable by his research as a psychiatrist at the Walter Reed Medical Center and nothing else derogatory was found that would have suggested that he was involved in terrorist activities or planning. U.S. Department of Justice, Federal Bureau of Investigation, "Investigation Continues Into Fort Hood Shooting," November 11, 2009.

[211] U.S. Department of Justice, Office of Inspector General, Audit Division, *Federal Bureau of Investigation's Terrorist Watchlist Nomination Practices*, Audit Report 09-25, May 2009, p. 11.

[212] Hasan reportedly purchased the Fabrique Nationale 5.7mm pistol that he used in the shootings on August 1, 2009. He also carried a .357 magnum revolver; however, it is unclear whether he fired the revolver.

---

renewed interest in the U.S. government's use of terrorist watch lists for firearms- and explosives-related background checks.[213]

Post-9/11 Modified NICS Procedures

Before February 2004, terrorist watch list checks were not part of the Brady background check process because being a suspected or known terrorist was and is not a disqualifying factor for firearms transfer/possession eligibility under federal or state law. As is the case today, to determine such eligibility, the National Instant Criminal Background Checks System (NICS) queries three databases maintained by the FBI. They include the National Crime Information Center (NCIC), the Interstate Identification Index (III), and the NICS index. The NICS index includes disqualifying records on persons that would not be included in the III or NCIC, for example, persons dishonorably discharged from the Armed Forces, adjudicated as a mental defective, or convicted of certain serious immigration violations, among others. The III contains criminal history records for persons arrested and convicted of felonies and certain serious misdemeanors. The NCIC contains law enforcement files on fugitives and persons subject to restraining orders, among other persons. NCIC also contains a file known as the Violent Gang and Terrorist Organization File (VGTOF). Prior to the 9/11 attacks, this file included *limited* information on known or suspected terrorists and gang members. NICS examiners were not informed of VGTOF hits, as such information was not considered relevant to determining firearms transfer/possession eligibility.

In November 2002, DOJ initiated a NICS transaction audit to determine whether prohibited aliens (non-citizens) were being improperly transferred firearms.[214] As part of this audit, NICS procedures were changed so that NICS examiners would be informed of VGTOF hits. Under Homeland Security Presidential Directive 6, moreover, the Administration initiated a broad-based review of the use of watch lists, among other terrorist identification and screening mechanisms.[215] In September 2003, the FBI-administered Terrorist Screening Center (TSC) was established and work was begun to improve and merge several watch lists maintained by the U.S. government into a consolidated Terrorist Screening Database (TSDB).[216] Following those efforts, TSDB lookout records from other agency watch lists were downloaded into VGTOF. By May 2007, VGTOF contained more than 100,000 records.[217] In 2009, the FBI created a separate file for "known and appropriately suspected terrorists (KST)" by splitting VGTOF into separate gang and terrorist files.[218] As of March 31, 2010, the KST included 278,219 terrorist watch list records.[219]

---

[213] Michael Bloomberg and Thomas Kean, "Enabling the Next Fort Hood? Congress's Curbs on Gun Data Hurt Investigations," *Washington Post*, November 27, 2009, p. A23.

[214] U.S. Government Accountability Office, *Gun Control and Terrorism: FBI Could Better Manage Firearm-Related Background Checks Involving Terrorist Watch List Records*, GAO-05-127, January 2005, p. 7.

[215] For further information, see CRS Report RL32366, *Terrorist Identification, Screening, and Tracking Under Homeland Security Presidential Directive 6*, by William J. Krouse.

[216] Ibid., p. 9.

[217] U.S. Department of Justice, Federal Bureau of Investigation, Criminal Justice Information Services (CJIS) Division, "NCIC Marks 40 Years of Serving Law Enforcement," *The CJIS Link: Criminal Justice Information Services that Connect Local, State, and Federal Law Enforcement*, vol. 10, no. 1, May 2007, p. 2.

[218] Daniel D. Roberts, Assistant Director, Criminal Justice Information Services, Federal Bureau of Investigation, Statement Before the Senate Committee on Homeland Security and Governmental Affairs, May 5, 2010, p. 1.

[219] Statistics provided by the FBI Office of Congressional Affairs to CRS on May 11, 2010.

In November 2003, DOJ directed the FBI to revise its NICS procedures to include measures to screen prospective firearms transferees and permittees against terrorist watch list records (KST, formerly VGTOF).[220] Effective February 2004, the Brady background check process was altered to include a terrorist watch list check and to alert NICS staff when a prospective firearms transferee or permit applicant is potentially identified as a known or suspected terrorist.[221] In the case of a watch list hit, NICS sends a delayed transfer (for up to three business days) response to the querying FFL or POC. If NICS examiners cannot find a prohibiting factor, they immediately contact the TSC and FBI Counterterrorism Division (CTD) to (1) validate the hit and (2) allow FBI Special Agents in the field to check for possible prohibiting factors. If no prohibiting factors are uncovered within the three-day period, a firearms dealer may proceed with the transaction at his discretion, but FBI counterterrorism officials continue to work the case for up to 90 days, during which time the background check is considered to be in an "open" status.[222]

If and when a transaction is approved, all identifying information submitted by or on behalf of the transferee is destroyed within 24 hours.[223] At the end of the 90-day period, if no prohibiting factor has been reported to the NICS Center, all records related to the NICS transaction are destroyed except for the NICS Transaction Number (NTN) and date of the transaction.[224] If the FFL proceeded with the transaction at his discretion following three business days and the applicant is found to be disqualified, then the ATF will be notified and a firearms retrieval action will be initiated in coordination with a JTTF.

NICS Record Retention

When Congress passed the Brady Act in 1994, the use of terrorist watch lists during firearms-related background checks was not considered. As a consequence, the Attorney General has no specific statutory authority to screen prospective gun buyers against terrorist watch list records. Nevertheless, the FBI adopted procedures to do this because being on such a list suggests that there may be an underlying factor that would bar a prospective background check applicant from possessing a firearm. Hence, a possible issue for Congress could be whether terrorist watch list checks should be incorporated statutorily into the Brady background checks for firearms.

In addition, a proviso attached to the FY2005 DOJ annual appropriation and every year thereafter requires that NICS-generated approved firearms transaction records be destroyed within 24 hours.[225] Nevertheless, as described above, the FBI has been retaining approved firearms transaction records for up to 90 days, if those records are related to terrorist watch list hits. Furthermore, information on the subjects of those checks are passed on to FBI investigators in the

---

[220] Ibid., p. 11.

[221] Dan Eggen, "FBI Gets More Time on Gun Buys," *Washington Post*, November 22, 2003, p. A05.

[222] U.S. Government Accountability Office, *Gun Control and Terrorism: FBI Could Better Manage Firearm-Related Background Checks Involving Terrorist Watch List Records*, GAO-05-127, January 2005, p. 32.

[223] 28 C.F.R. §25.9(b)(1)(iii).

[224] 28 C.F.R. §25.9(b)(1)(ii).

[225] For FY2009, see §511 of the Omnibus Appropriations Act, 2009, (P.L. 111-8, 123 Stat. 596). For FY2010, see also §511 of the Consolidated Appropriations Act, 2010 (P.L. 111-117, 123 Stat. 3151). For FY2011, the Department of Defense and Full-Year Continuing Appropriations Act, 2011 (P.L. 112-10) carried this requirement forward from FY2010. For FY2012, The Minibus Appropriations Act (H.R. 2112) includes a §511 that not only includes the "24 hour" destruction requirement, but it also includes "futurity" language, which makes the provision permanent law, as opposed to an annual appropriations restriction. The President has signed this bill into law (P.L. 112-55).

---

field. While the NICS records are eventually destroyed for non-denials, it is unknown what happens to the information generated by NICS-related terrorist watch list hits that are passed on to the FBI CTD and Special Agents in the field, who are usually assigned to Joint Terrorism Task Forces. Information about those firearms transactions is possibly recorded and stored electronically in the FBI's investigative case files.

In the Brady Act, however, there is a provision that prohibits the (1) transfer of any Brady system record to any other federal or state agency, or (2) the use of the Brady system as a national registry of firearms or firearms owners.[226] In light of the former prohibition, a second issue for Congress could be whether to grant the FBI greater authority to maintain and access NICS records for the purposes of counterterrorism, or should existing statutory limitations that were arguably designed to prevent the maintenance of and access to such records be strengthened. In light of the first two issues, it follows that a third issue for Congress could be whether the Attorney General should be given explicit authority to deny firearms transfers to watch-listed persons on a case-by-case basis, or should all known or suspected terrorists be statutorily prohibited from possessing firearms and explosives.[227]

Legislation in the 110th Congress and DOJ Draft Proposal

As described above, although watch-listed persons may be the subject of ongoing foreign intelligence, national security, and criminal investigations, they may not be persons prohibited from possessing firearms or explosives under current law. As subsequent events would indicate, DOJ concluded that it was limited under current law in its authority to use terrorist watch lists as part of the background check processes to deny firearms and explosives transfers to known or suspected terrorists. In hearings before the House Committee on the Judiciary, Attorney General

---

[226] For example, subsection 103(i) of the Brady Act (P.L. 103-159; 107 Stat. 1542) includes the following provision: PROHIBITION RELATING TO ESTABLISHMENT OF REGISTRATION SYSTEMS WITH RESPOECT TO FIREARMS. – No department, agency, officer, or employee of the United States may – (1) require that any record or portion thereof generated by the system established under this section be recorded at or transferred to a facility owned, managed, or controlled by the United States or any State or political subdivision thereof; or (2) use the system established under this section to establish any system for the registration of firearms, firearm owners, or firearm transaction or disposition, except with respect to persons, prohibited by section 922 (g) or (n) of title 18, United States Code or State law, from receiving a firearm.

[227] In the 109th Congress (2005-2006), several pieces of legislation were introduced that were related to NICS background checks and terrorist watch lists. In March 2005, Senator Lautenberg and Representative John Conyers introduced the Terrorist Apprehension and Record Retention Act of 2005 (S. 578/H.R. 1225), a bill that would have (1) required that the FBI, along with appropriate federal and state counterterrorism officials, be notified immediately when NICS background checks indicated that a person seeking to obtain a firearm was a known or suspected terrorist; (2) required that the FBI coordinate the response to such occurrences; and (3) authorized the retention of all related records for at least 10 years.

In addition, Representative Peter King introduced H.R. 1168, a bill that would have required the Attorney General to promulgate regulations to preserve records of terrorist- and gang-related matches during such background checks until they had been provided to the FBI. Representative Carolyn McCarthy introduced H.R. 1195, a bill that would have made it unlawful to transfer a firearm to a person who was on the "No Fly" lists maintained by TSA.

In summation, two of those proposals (S. 578/H.R. 1225 and H.R. 1168) addressed the retention of approved firearm background check records that are related to terrorist watch list matches. The other bill (H.R. 1195) addressed the issue of whether a known or suspected terrorist on one government watch list in particular should be barred from possessing firearms. Neither of these bills, however, addressed the other underlying issue of how long the total number of approved firearm transfer records should be retained and, if retained, whether they should be searched to determine whether known or suspected terrorists had previously obtained firearms.

Alberto Gonzales was questioned several times by Members of Congress about NICS procedures and terrorist watch list hits.

> Representative Chris Van Hollen: "Does it make sense to you that we stop a person from boarding the airline in order to protect the public safety, [but] that an individual can turn around, get in their car, go to the local gun shop and buy 20 semiautomatic assault weapons?"
>
> Attorney General Gonzales: "I think we should be doing everything we can to ensure that people [who] are in fact terrorists shouldn't have weapons in this country, the truth of the matter is. But unless they are disabled [disqualified] from having a weapon under the statute there's not much that we can do other than maybe try and get them out of the country or, by the way, to see if there's any disability under the statute that would allow us to deny them a firearm."[228]

In 2005, then Attorney General Gonzales directed the DOJ to form a working group to review federal gun laws—particularly in regard to NICS background checks—to examine whether additional authority should be sought to prevent firearms transfers to known or suspected terrorists.[229] Nearly two years later, on April 25, 2007, DOJ proposed legislation that would give the Attorney General authority to deny a firearm transfer, state-issued firearms permit, or explosive license to any person found "to be or have been engaged in conduct constituting, in preparation for, in aid of, or related to terrorism."[230] In the 110th Congress (2007-2008), Senator Lautenberg and Representative King introduced this proposal (S. 1237/H.R. 2074), but no further action was taken on either bill.

Legislation in the 111th Congress, GAO Follow-Up Report, and Senate Hearing

In the 111th Congress (2009-2010), several bills were introduced that would have addressed firearms- and explosives-related background checks and terrorist watch list checks. Senator Lautenberg and Representative King reintroduced their bill that was based on the DOJ draft proposal (S. 1317 and H.R. 2159). Representative McCarthy reintroduced her bill, newly titled the No Fly, No Buy Act of 2009, that would have allowed the Attorney General to deny firearms to persons who are on the TSA's No Fly terrorist watch list (H.R. 2401). And, Senator Lautenberg introduced a bill that would have allowed the Attorney General to maintain NICS records on approved transfers that were also related terrorist watch list hits (S. 2820). In addition, GAO provided Congress with updated data on NICS-related terrorist watch list hits, lending renewed impetus to the reintroduction of the DOJ draft proposal. And, the November 2009 Fort Hood shootings renewed interest in terrorist watch list records and firearms-related background checks.

---

[228] *USA Patriot Act: A Review for the Purpose of Reauthorization: Hearing Before H. Comm. on the Judiciary*, 109th Cong. 81-82 (Apr. 6, 2005) (Testimony of Alberto Gonzales, Attorney General, Department of Justice).

[229] U.S. Department of Justice, Office of Legislative Affairs, Letter to the Honorable Richard B. Cheney, President, United States Senate, from Richard A. Hertling Acting Assistant Attorney General, February 13, 2007, http://lautenberg.senate.gov/assets/terrorgap/Feb_2007_DOJ_Reply.pdf; Letter to Honorable Robert S. Mueller, III, Director of the Federal Bureau of Investigation and Honrable Alberto Gonzales, Attorney General, November 1, 2006, http://lautenberg.senate.gov/assets/terrorgap/2006_Lautenberg_Biden_Letter.pdf.

[230] This proposal was drafted by the Department of Justice for consideration by Congress. *See* U.S. Dep't of Justice, Office of Legislative Affairs, Letter to the Honorable Richard B. Cheney, President, United States Senate, from Richard A. Hertling Acting Assistant Attorney General, April 25, 2007, http://lautenberg.senate.gov/assets/terrorgap/Cheney_DOJ_Drafted_Bill_Re_Dangerous_Terrorists_Act_2007.pdf.

GAO Follow-Up Report on NICS-Related Terrorist Watch List Hits (May 2009)

Nearly four years after the first GAO report, GAO issued a follow-up report on NICS-related terrorist watch list hits in May 2009. GAO reported that from February 2004 through February 2009 there were

- 963 NICS background checks that resulted in terrorist watch list matches and, of those checks, about 90% (865) were allowed to proceed and a firearms or explosives transfer may have occurred;

- however, only one explosives background check resulted in a proceed with transaction; and

- of the 10% that resulted in denials (98), the denials were based on felony convictions, illegal immigration status, fugitive from justice status, and the unlawful use of, or addiction to, a controlled substance. All of these denials involved firearms, as opposed to explosives.[231]

In this report, GAO also recommended that if Congress should move forward with legislation providing the Attorney General with the discretionary authority to deny a firearms transfer or permit, or an explosives license/permit, based on a terrorist watch list hit, then, consideration should be given to including a provision in that legislation that would require the Attorney General to promulgate guidelines that would delineate under what circumstances such authority could be evoked. Following this report, Representative King and Senator Lautenberg reintroduced the DOJ draft proposal as nearly identical bills (H.R. 2159 and S. 1317), which supporters dubbed the "Terror Gap" proposal.

Senate Homeland Security and Governmental Affairs Committee Hearing

On May 5, 2010, the Senate Committee on Homeland Security and Governmental Affairs held a hearing on "Terrorists and Guns: The Nature of the Threat and Proposed Reforms." GAO testified about measures taken by the FBI to improve firearms and explosives background checks for counterterrorism purposes.[232] GAO reported that from February 2004 through February 2010, there were 1,228 positive encounters with individuals watch-listed as terrorists through NICS related firearms or explosives transactions.[233] These encounters involved 650 individuals because 450 of these individuals were involved in multiple transactions.[234] Six of these individuals were involved in 10 or more transactions.[235] In 1,119 encounters, the transactions were allowed to proceed.[236] In 109 encounters, the transactions were denied.[237] From March 2009 to February

---

[231] U.S. Government Accountability Office, GAO-09-125R, *Firearm and Explosive Background Checks Involving Terrorist Watch List Records* 8 (May 2009).

[232] U.S. Government Accountability Office, *Terrorist Watchlist Screening: FBI Has Enhanced Its Use of Information from Firearm and Explosives Background Checks to Support Counterterrorism Efforts*, GAO-10-703T, May 5, 2010.

[233] Ibid. p. 5.

[234] Ibid.

[235] Ibid.

[236] Ibid.

[237] Ibid.

2009, moreover, there were 272 positive encounters and all of the transactions were allowed to proceed, including one that involved explosives.[238]

Senator Joseph Lieberman, chair of the committee, noted that firearms had been used in at least two deadly terrorist plots perpetrated by Muslim extremists. Those incidents included the Fort Hood shootings noted above and the June 2009 Little Rock, AR, recruiting center shootings, where two U.S. servicemen were shot—one was killed and the other wounded. In several other thwarted plots, conspirators were arrested for planning to use firearms to attack servicemen at Fort Dix, NJ, in 2006 and the Quantico, VA, Marine base in 2009.[239] Senator Lindsey Graham, however, voiced opposition to the Terror Gap proposal. He maintained that denying a firearms transfer based upon a felony conviction in a lawful court was fundamentally different from doing so based on a terrorist watch list record that was created by an investigator or intelligence analyst.[240]

Legislation in the 112th Congress

In the 112th Congress, Senator Lautenberg and Representative King have reintroduced the Terror Gap proposal (S. 34 and H.R. 1506). As in the preceding two Congresses, these nearly identical bills are based upon the April 2007 DOJ proposed legislative language.

ATF Modernization Act

On at least two occasions during the 111th Congress, the Senate Judiciary Committee postponed hearings on the Bureau of Alcohol, Tobacco, Firearms and Explosives Reform and Firearms Modernization Act (S. 941). Senator Mike Crapo and Senator Patrick Leahy, chair of the Judiciary Committee, introduced this bill on April 30, 2009. Representatives Steve King and Zack Space introduced a companion bill (H.R. 2296). In regard to regulating federally licensed firearms dealers, this proposal would have

- established a two tier, graduated penalty system for violations characterized as being of a minor or serious nature;

- established a process by which ATF licensing decisions could be reviewed by an administrative law judge;

- required the Attorney General to issue guidelines governing ATF investigations of GCA violations; and

- defined the "willful" standard of intent to mean "knowingly and intentionally" disregarding a "legal duty."

Proponents for this proposal argue that these provisions would allow federal firearms licensees greater opportunity to address non-substantive recordkeeping issues that under current law could lead to the revocation of their licenses. Opponents argue that relaxing such provisions would weaken ATF authority and efforts to reduce the number of "kitchen table top" dealers, who are

---

[238] Ibid., p. 2.

[239] U.S. Senate, Senate Committee on Homeland Security and Governmental Affairs, *Hearing on Terrorist Threat and Guns*, 111th Congress, 2nd Session, May 5, 2010 (*CQ* Congressional Transcripts).

[240] Ibid.

not substantively engaged in the business and, hence, are ineligible for such licenses, and "rogue" dealers, who are not adequately controlling and accounting for their firearms inventories.[241] Additional provisions in the bill would have addressed several other firearms-related issues concerning machine guns, firearms parts, and handgun possession of a minor in the presence of a parent or legal guardian. In the 112th Congress, Representative Steve King and Senator Mike Crapo have reintroduced this proposal (H.R. 1093/S. 835).

Gun Shows and Private Firearms Transfers

Federal law does not regulate gun shows specifically. Federal law regulating firearms transfers, however, is applicable to such transfers at gun shows. Federal firearms licensees—those licensed by the federal government to manufacture, import, or deal in firearms—are required to conduct background checks on non-licensed persons seeking to obtain firearms from them, by purchase or exchange. Conversely, non-licensed persons—those persons who transfer firearms but who do not meet the statutory test of being engaged in the business—are not required to conduct such checks. To some, this may appear to be an incongruity in the law. Why, they ask, should licensees be required to conduct background checks at gun shows but not non-licensees? To those opposed to further federal regulation of firearms, it may appear to be a continuance of the status quo (i.e., non-interference by the federal government into private firearms transfers within state lines). On the other hand, those seeking to increase federal regulation of firearms may view the absence of background checks for firearms transfers between non-licensed/private persons as a loophole in the law that needs to be closed. A possible issue for Congress is whether federal regulation of firearms should be expanded to include private firearms transfers at gun shows and other similar venues.

Among gun show-related proposals, there are two basic models. The first model is based on a bill (S. 443) that was introduced in the 106th Congress by Senator Lautenberg, who successfully offered this proposal as an amendment to the Senate-passed Violent and Repeat Juvenile Offender Act (S. 254). Several Members introduced variations of the Lautenberg bill in the 107th Congress. In the 108th Congress, Representative Conyers—ranking minority Member of the Judiciary Committee—introduced H.R. 260, which was very similar to the Lautenberg bill. In addition, former Senator Daschle introduced the Justice Enhancement and Domestic Security Act of 2003 (S. 22), which included gun show language that was similar to the Lautenberg bill. The second model is based on a bill (S. 890) introduced in the 107th Congress by Senators McCain and Lieberman.[242] In the 108th Congress, Senator McCain reintroduced this proposal as well (S. 1807). And, Representative Michael Castle introduced a similar gun show proposal (H.R. 3832).

---

[241] In the 109th Congress, Representative Howard Coble, chair of the House Judiciary Subcommittee on Crime, Terrorism, and Homeland Security, and Representative Robert Scott, the subcommittee's ranking minority Member, introduced the ATFE Modernization and Reform Act of 2006 (H.R. 5092) on April 5, 2006. H.R. 5092 was approved by the Crime subcommittee on May 3, 2006. The House Judiciary Committee ordered this bill reported on September 7, and a written report was filed on September 21 (H.Rept. 109-672). The House passed this bill on September 26, 2006, by a recorded vote of 277-131 (Roll no. 476), but no further action was taken on this bill. Also see U.S. Congress, House Committee on the Judiciary, Subcommittee on Crime, Terrorism, and Homeland Security, *The Bureau of Alcohol, Tobacco, Firearms and Explosives (BATFE): Gun Show Enforcement (Parts 1 and 2)*, 109th Cong., 2nd sess., February 15 and 28, 2006, H.Hrg. 109-123 (Washington: GPO, 2006).

[242] For further information, see CRS Report RL32249, *Gun Control: Proposals to Regulate Gun Shows*, by William J. Krouse and T.J. Halstead (available upon request).

Also in the 108th Congress, on March 2, 2004, during consideration of the Protection of Lawful Commerce in Arms Act (S. 1805), the Senate passed a gun show-related amendment (S.Amdt. 2636) offered by Senator McCain by a yea-nay vote of 53-46 (Record Vote Number: 25). However, the bill's floor manager, Senator Larry Craig, pulled this bill from further floor consideration before a final vote could be taken on the measure rather than risk passage of a bill that included gun control and assault weapons ban provisions (the latter provision is described below).

In the 109th Congress, Representative Castle reintroduced his proposal (H.R. 3540), but a similar measure was not introduced in the Senate. In the 110th Congress, Representative Castle and Senator Lautenberg reintroduced separate gun show proposals (H.R. 96 and S. 2577). Senator Biden included similar provisions in the Crime Control and Prevention Act of 2007 (S. 2237). In the 111th Congress, Senator Lautenberg and Representative Castle again reintroduced similar measures that would have required background checks for private firearms transfers at guns shows (S. 843 and H.R. 2324). In the 112th Congress, Senator Lautenberg has reintroduced this measure (S. 35) and Representative McCarthy has introduced a companion measure (H.R. 591).

Expired Semiautomatic Assault Weapons Ban

In 1994, Congress banned for 10 years the possession, transfer, or further domestic manufacture of semiautomatic assault weapons (SAWs) and large-capacity ammunition feeding devices (LCAFDs) that hold more than 10 rounds that were not legally owned or available prior to the date of enactment (September 13, 1994). The SAW-LCAFD ban expired on September 13, 2004. The SAW ban statute classified a rifle as a semiautomatic assault weapon if it was able to accept a detachable magazine and included two or more of the following five characteristics: (1) a folding or telescoping stock, (2) a pistol grip, (3) a bayonet mount, (4) a muzzle flash suppressor or threaded barrel capable of accepting such a suppressor, or (5) a grenade launcher.[243] There were similar definitions for pistols and shotguns that were classified as semiautomatic assault weapons.[244] Semiautomatic assault weapons that were legally owned prior to the ban were not restricted and remained available for transfer under applicable federal and state laws. Opponents of the ban argue that the statutorily defined characteristics of a semiautomatic assault weapon were largely cosmetic, and that these weapons were potentially no more lethal than other semiautomatic firearms that were designed to accept a detachable magazine and were equal or superior in terms of ballistics and other performance characteristics. Proponents of the ban argue that semiautomatic military-style firearms, particularly those capable of accepting large-capacity ammunition feeding devices, had and have no place in the civilian gun stock.

During and following World War II, *assault rifles* were developed to provide a lighter infantry weapon that could fire more rounds, more rapidly (increased capacity and rate of fire). To increase capacity of fire, detachable self-feeding magazines were developed. These rifles were usually designed to be fired in fully automatic mode, meaning that once the trigger is pulled, the weapon continues to fire rapidly until all the rounds in the magazine are expended or the trigger is released. Often these rifles were also designed with a "select fire" feature that allowed them to be fired in short bursts (e.g., three rounds per pull of the trigger), or in semiautomatic mode (i.e., one

---

[243] 18 U.S.C. §921(a)(30)(B).

[244] 18 U.S.C. §921(a)(30)(C) and (D).

round per pull of the trigger), as well as in fully automatic mode. By comparison, semiautomatic firearms, including semiautomatic assault weapons, fire one round per pull of the trigger.

According to a 1997 survey of 203,300 state and federal prisoners who had been armed during the commission of the crimes for which they were incarcerated, fewer than 1 in 50, or less than 2%, used, carried, or possessed a semiautomatic assault weapon or machine gun.[245] Under current law, any firearm that can be fired in fully automatic mode or in multi-round bursts is classified as a "machine gun" and must be registered with the federal government under the National Firearms Act of 1934. Furthermore, it is illegal to assemble a machine gun with legally or illegally obtained parts. The population of legally owned machine guns has been frozen since 1986, and they were not covered by the semiautomatic assault weapons ban.

In the 108th Congress, proposals were introduced to extend or make permanent the ban, whereas other proposals were made to modify the definition of "semiautomatic assault weapon" to cover a greater number of firearms by reducing the number of features that would constitute such firearms, and expand the list of certain makes and models of firearms that are statutorily enumerated as banned. A proposal (S. 1034) introduced by Senator Dianne Feinstein would have made the ban permanent as would have a proposal (H.R. 2038/S. 1431) introduced by Representative McCarthy and Senator Lautenberg. The latter measure, however, would have modified the definition and expanded the list of banned weapons. Senator Feinstein also introduced measures that would have extended the ban for 10 years (S. 2109/S. 2498). In addition, on March 2, 2004, the Senate passed an amendment to the gun industry liability bill (S. 1805) that would have extended the ban for 10 years, but the Senate did not pass this bill.[246]

In the 109th Congress, Senator Dianne Feinstein introduced a bill that would have reinstated previous law for 10 years (S. 620). Representative McCarthy and Senator Lautenberg reintroduced their bills to make the ban permanent (H.R. 1312/S. 645).

In the 110th Congress, Representative McCarthy reintroduced a similar proposal (H.R. 1022) and another measure (H.R. 1859) that would prohibit the transfer of a semiautomatic assault weapon with a large-capacity ammunition feeding device, among other things. Representative Mark Steven Kirk introduced the Assault Weapons Ban Reauthorization Act of 2008 (H.R. 6257). Senator Biden included provisions to reauthorize the ban in the Crime Control and Prevention Act of 2007 (S. 2237).

In the wake of the Tucson shootings, Representative McCarthy introduced a measure that would reinstate the large capacity ammunition feeding device ban (H.R. 308). Senator Lautenberg introduced a similar measure (S. 32).

---

[245] For further information, see Caroline Wolf Harlow, *Firearm Use by Offenders*, at http://bjs.ojp.usdoj.gov/index.cfm?ty=pbdetail&iid=940.

[246] For further information, see CRS Report RL32077, *The Assault Weapons Ban: Legal Challenges and Legislative Issues*, by T. J. Halstead; and CRS Report RL32585, *Semiautomatic Assault Weapons Ban*, by William J. Krouse.

Long-Range .50 Caliber Rifles[247]

In the 109th Congress, legislation was introduced to regulate more strictly certain .50 caliber rifles. Some of these rifles are chambered to fire a relatively large round originally designed for the Browning Machine Gun (BMG) and have been adopted by the U.S. military as long-range "sniper" rifles. Gun control advocates argue that these firearms have little sporting, hunting, or recreational purpose. They maintain that these rifles could be used to shoot down aircraft, rupture pressurized chemical tanks, or penetrate armored personnel carriers. Gun control opponents counter that these rifles are expensive, cumbersome, and rarely, if ever, used to commit crimes. Furthermore, they maintain that these rifles were first developed for long-range marksmanship competitions and then adopted by the military as sniper rifles.

The Fifty Caliber Sniper Weapons Regulation Act of 2005 (S. 935), introduced by Senator Dianne Feinstein, would have amended the National Firearms Act (NFA)[248] to regulate ".50 caliber sniper weapons" in the same fashion as short-barreled shotguns and silencers by levying taxes on the manufacture and transfer of such firearms and by requiring owner and firearms registration. In the 110th Congress, Senator Feinstein introduced a similar measure (S. 1331).

The other proposal introduced by Representative James Moran, the 50 Caliber Sniper Rifle Reduction Act (H.R. 654), also would have amended the NFA to include those weapons, but it would have also amended the Gun Control Act[249] to effectively freeze the population of those weapons legally available to private persons and to prohibit any further transfer of those firearms. In other words, H.R. 654 would have grandfathered-in existing rifles but would have banned their further transfer. Consequently, the proposal would have eventually eliminated those rifles all together from the civilian gun stock. It would have been likely that covered .50 caliber rifles would have had to be destroyed or handed over to the ATF as contraband when the legal firearm owner died or wanted to give up the firearm. H.R. 654 included no compensation provision for rifles destroyed or handed over to the federal government.

Furthermore, both proposals (S. 935 and H.R. 654) would have defined ".50 caliber sniper weapon" to mean "a rifle capable of firing center-fire cartridge in .50 caliber, .50 BMG caliber, any other variant of .50 caliber or any metric equivalent of such calibers." Many rifles, and even some handguns, are chambered to fire .50 caliber ammunition, meaning the projectile is about one-half inch in diameter. Opponents of this legislation note that this definition was very broad and would have likely covered .50 caliber rifles that would not be considered "long-range" or "sniper" rifles. The .50 BMG caliber round, on the other hand, is an exceptionally large cartridge (projectile and casing), which was once used almost exclusively as a heavy machine gun round. Representative Moran also offered an amendment to the FY2006 Department of Commerce appropriations bill (H.R. 2862) that would have prohibited the use of funding provided under that bill to process licenses to export .50 caliber rifles, but that amendment was not adopted by the House.

---

[247] For further information, see CRS Report RS22151, *Long-Range Fifty Caliber Rifles: Should They Be More Strictly Regulated?*, by William J. Krouse.

[248] 26 U.S.C., Chapter 53, §5801 et seq.

[249] 18 U.S.C., Chapter 44, §921 et seq.

Appendix A. Legislation in the 111ᵗʰ Congress

The 111ᵗʰ Congress revisited several issues previously considered in the 110ᵗʰ Congress. For example, Congress considered amendments to DC voting rights bills that would have further overturned DC gun laws (S. 160 and H.R. 157). In addition, Congress passed several other gun-related provisions included in enacted legislation that address

- carrying firearms on public lands (P.L. 111-24),

- transporting firearms in passenger luggage on Amtrak trains (P.L. 111-117),

- widening law enforcement off-duty concealed carry privileges (P.L. 111-272), and

- prohibiting higher health care premiums for gun owners (P.L. 111-148).

The 111ᵗʰ Congress also reconsidered or newly considered several other provisions that were not enacted:

- gun rights restoration for veterans previously deemed to be mentally incompetent (S. 669 and H.R. 6132),

- interstate reciprocity of concealed carry privileges (S. 1390 and S. 845),

- firearms possession in public housing (H.R. 3045 and H.R. 4868), and

- the treatment of firearms under bankruptcy proceedings (H.R. 5827/S. 3654).

Constitutionality of DC Handgun Ban and Related Legislation

On June 26, 2008, the Supreme Court issued its decision in *District of Columbia v. Heller* on the constitutionality of a DC law that banned handguns for 32 years, among other things. Passed by the DC Council on June 26, 1976, the DC handgun ban required that all firearms within the District be registered and all owners be licensed, and it prohibited the registration of handguns after September 24, 1976. In a 5-4 decision, the Supreme Court found the handgun ban to be unconstitutional because it violated an individual's right under the Second Amendment to possess a handgun in his home for lawful purposes such as self-defense.[250]

DC Council Passes Emergency Law

On July 15, 2008, the DC Council passed a temporary, emergency law that allowed residents through a registration/certificate process to keep a handgun in their home as long as that firearm had a capacity of fewer than 12 rounds of ammunition and was not loadable from a magazine in the handgrip, which in effect limited legal handguns under the temporary law to revolvers as opposed to semiautomatic pistols. The emergency law also continued to require that handguns be kept unloaded and disassembled, or trigger locked, unless an attack in a home was imminent or underway. Pro-gun groups immediately criticized the council's emergency law for not being in the "spirit" of the Supreme Court's decision because it continued to ban semiautomatic pistols

---

[250] For legal analysis, see CRS Report R41750, *The Second Amendment: An Overview of District of Columbia v. Heller and McDonald v. City of Chicago*, by Vivian S. Chu.

and did not fully roll back the trigger lock requirement. Since the initial emergency law was passed, the DC Council has passed several other pieces of similar temporary, emergency laws related to the *Heller* decision. These laws include new firearms-related provisions that were also included in permanent legislation passed by the DC Council that is described below.

Legislation Related to DC Gun Laws[251]

Several Members of Congress were dissatisfied with the DC Council's temporary law. On July 24, 2008, Representative Mike Ross filed a motion to discharge the Rules Committee from consideration of H.Res. 1331, a resolution that would have provided for the consideration of a bill to restore Second Amendment rights in the District of Columbia (H.R. 1399).[252] This bill was similar to previous bills introduced by Representative Mark Souder and Senators Kay Bailey Hutchison and Orrin Hatch in previous congresses. Representative Ross introduced H.R. 1399 in the 110th Congress for himself and Representative Souder on March 27, 2007, and Senator Hutchison introduced a companion measure (S. 1001) on March 28, 2007.

In the 110th Congress, Representative Travis Childers introduced a similar bill (H.R. 6691) on July 31, 2008. All three bills would have amended the DC Code to

- limit the Council's authority to regulate firearms;

- remove semiautomatic firearms that can fire more than 12 rounds without manually reloading from the definition of "machine gun";

- amend the registration requirements so that they do not apply to handguns, but only to sawed-off shotguns, machine guns, and short-barreled rifles;

- remove restrictions on ammunition possession;

- repeal requirements that DC residents keep firearms in their possession unloaded and disassembled, or bound by a trigger lock;

- repeal firearms registration requirements generally; and

- repeal certain criminal penalties for possessing or carrying unregistered firearms.

Representatives John Dingell, John Tanner, and Mike Ross reportedly negotiated an agreement with the House leadership to consider H.R. 6691 in early September.[253] H.R. 6691 included language that stated as a congressional finding that DC officials "have indicated their intention to continue to unduly restrict lawful firearm possession and use by citizens of the District." H.R. 6691 also included a provision that would have allowed DC residents to purchase firearms from federally licensed gun dealers in Virginia and Maryland.

---

[251] Foreshadowing the contentiousness of the DC gun ban issue, Representative Lamar Smith had previously scuttled the District of Columbia House Voting Rights Act of 2007 (H.R. 1433) on March 22, 2007, when he offered a motion to recommit the bill to the House Oversight and Government Reform Committee for consideration of an amendment to repeal portions of the DC handgun ban. Rather than vote on the motion, debate on H.R. 1433 was postponed indefinitely. Jonathan Allen, "Gun-Rights Gambit Sidetracks D.C. House Vote," *CQ Today*, March 22, 2007; and for further information on H.R. 1433, see CRS Report RL33830, *District of Columbia Voting Representation in Congress: An Analysis of Legislative Proposals*, by Eugene Boyd.

[252] Under the Home Rule Act (P.L. 93-198), Congress has reserved for itself the authority to legislate for the District.

[253] Keith Perine and Seth Stern, "House Democrats Plan Vote To Roll Back D.C. Gun Laws," *CQ Today Online News*, August 5, 2008.

On September 9, 2008, the House Oversight and Government Reform Committee held a hearing on the possible effects H.R. 6691 might have on the District. On the same day, Representative Eleanor Holmes Norton introduced H.R. 6842, a bill that would have required the DC mayor and Council to ensure that regulations were promulgated that would have been consistent with the *Heller* decision. On September 15, 2008, the House Oversight and Government Reform Committee reported H.R. 6842 (H.Rept. 110-843). On September 17, 2008, however, the House amended H.R. 6842 with the text of H.R. 6691 and passed the Childers' bill.

DC Council Passes Permanent Legislation

On December 16, 2008, the DC Council passed the Firearms Control Amendment Act of 2008 (FCAA; B17-0843) and the Inoperable Pistol Amendment Act of 2008 (IPAA; B17-0593).[254] Mayor Adrian Fenty signed the FCAA into law on January 28, 2009 (L17-0372). This bill was transmitted to Congress on February 10, 2009. From the day of transmittal, Congress had 30 legislative days to review this bill under the DC Home Rule Act (according to the District of Columbia). Among other things, this law amends the DC Code to

- adopt the federal definition of "machine gun," which does not include semiautomatic pistols;

- prohibit the possession and registration of "assault weapons" and rifles capable of firing .50 caliber Browning Machine Gun (BMG) rounds; and

- require that all firearms made after January 1, 2011, be microstamped.[255]

Many provisions of this law, including the assault weapons ban and the microstamping provisions, were modeled after California state law.

Mayor Fenty signed IPAA into law on January 16, 2009 (L17-0388). It was transmitted to Congress on February 4, 2009. Because the bill includes penalty provisions, Congress had 60 legislative days to review this bill under the DC Home Rule Act. Among other things, this permanent legislation amends the DC Code to

- criminalize the possession of inoperable firearms;

- criminalize the discharge of firearms;

- prohibit carrying a rifle or shotgun;

- allow for the transportation of firearms under the same conditions as permitted under federal law; and

- change the waiting period to purchase a firearm from 48 hours to 10 days.

---

[254] For further information on these bills, as well as the Ensign amendment, see CRS Report R40474, *DC Gun Laws and Proposed Amendments*, by Vivian S. Chu.

[255] Microstamping is an emerging technology by which a firearm's serial number is engraved microscopically with a laser onto the breech face or firing pin of a firearm. When the firearm is fired, the serial number is "stamped" upon the cartridge casing. If a microstamped cartridge is subsequently recovered at a crime scene, the firearm's serial number could potentially yield additional leads for law enforcement.

DC Voting Rights and Gun Laws in the 111ᵗʰ Congress

On February 26, 2009, Senator John Ensign successfully amended (S.Amdt. 576) the District of Columbia House Voting Rights Act of 2009 (S. 160) by a yea-nay vote of 62-36 (Record Vote Number 72) with language that would have overturned certain DC guns laws and prevent the District from legislating in these areas in the future. The Senate passed this bill on the same day by a yea-nay vote of 61-37 (Record Vote Number 73).[256] This bill was tabled while the House leadership attempted to negotiate an end to the impasse over the DC gun laws and bring its version of the DC voting rights bill (H.R. 157) to the floor.[257] In April 2010, efforts were made to revive the voting rights bill, but some Members prepared amendments to overturn the city's gun laws. Consequently, Members managing the DC voting rights bill postponed further consideration rather than risk passage of amendments that would overturn the city's gun laws.[258] Senator John McCain and Representative Travis Childers introduced their amendments as stand-alone bills, the Second Amendment Enforcement Act (S. 3265/H.R. 5162). In the 112ᵗʰ Congress, Representative Mike Ross has introduced a proposal to restore Second Amendment rights in the District of Columbia (H.R. 645).

Constitutionality of the Chicago Handgun Ban

On June 28, 2010, the Supreme Court issued its 5-4 decision in *McDonald v. City of Chicago* and found that the individual right to lawfully possess a firearm for the purposes of self-defense under the Second Amendment applied to the states by way of the Fourteenth Amendment.[259] Although the *McDonald* decision arguably nullified the Chicago handgun ban by limiting a state, city, or local government's ability to prohibit handguns outright, it does not delineate what would constitute permissible gun control laws under the Second Amendment. Indeed, the Supreme Court remanded the Chicago handgun ban back to the Seventh Circuit Court of Appeals for a rehearing. Consequently, the delineation of permissible gun laws will likely be developed in future cases. Nevertheless, the city of Chicago has reportedly adopted handgun regulations that are similar to those adopted by the District of Columbia. These regulations allow eligible residents to register one operable handgun per household, but in most cases that handgun must be locked and rendered inoperable, and it cannot be carried outside of the home.[260]

Public Lands and Firearms Possession and Use

In the 111ᵗʰ Congress, Senator Tom Coburn successfully amended the Credit CARD Act of 2009 (H.R. 627) with a provision (S.Amdt. 1067) that allows private persons to carry firearms in national parks and wildlife refuges (effective February 22, 2010). This amendment passed by a vote of 67 to 29 (Record Vote Number 188) on May 12, 2009. Under H.Res. 456, the House voted

---

[256] For more information, see CRS Report R40474, *DC Gun Laws and Proposed Amendments*, by Vivian S. Chu.

[257] Edward Epstein and Michael Teitelbaum, "Hoyer Expresses Optimism About Chance D.C. Vote Bill Will Come to Floor," *CQ Today*, March 24, 2009.

[258] Ann E. Marimow and Ben Pershing, "District Voting Rights Scuttled: 'The Price Was Too High' Amendment Would Have Repealed D.C. Gun Laws," *Washington Post*, April 21, 2010, p. B01.

[259] For legal analysis, see CRS Report R41750, *The Second Amendment: An Overview of District of Columbia v. Heller and McDonald v. City of Chicago*, by Vivian S. Chu.

[260] Dave Workman, "Chicago Adopts New Gun Regs, Lawsuit Filed," *New Gun Week*, August 1, 2010, p. 1.

---

on the Coburn amendment as a separate measure and passed it by a vote of 279 to 147. President Barack Obama signed H.R. 627 into law on May 22, 2009 (P.L. 111-24).

Previously, in the 110th Congress during consideration of a public land bill (S. 2483), Senator Coburn offered but later withdrew an amendment (S.Amdt. 3967) that would have overturned federal regulations that prohibit visitors to parks and wildlife refuges managed by the National Park Service (NPS)[261] and Fish and Wildlife Service (FWS)[262] from possessing operable and loaded firearms. While these regulations were last revised substantively in 1981 and 1983, similar firearms restrictions were promulgated in the 1930s in an effort to curb poaching and other illegal activities. There are exceptions for hunting and marksmanship under current law. Since the 1980s, however, many states have passed laws that allow persons to carry concealed handguns for personal protection. Although 48 states have "concealed carry" laws, only 24 of those states reportedly allow concealed handguns to be carried in state parks.[263]

On April 30, 2008, in part at the urging of some Members of Congress, the Department of the Interior (DOI) published proposed regulations that would authorize the possession of loaded and concealed firearms, as long as carrying those firearms in that fashion would be legal under the laws of the states where the public lands are located.[264] While the initial comment period was scheduled to end on June 30, 2008, it was extended until August 8, 2008.[265] DOI reported receiving approximately 90,000 comments on those proposed regulations. Final regulations were issued on December 10, 2008.[266] Those regulations took effect on January 9, 2009. However, on March 19, a U.S. District Judge issued a preliminary injunction on the regulations in a lawsuit brought by three groups: the Brady Campaign to Prevent Gun Violence, the National Parks Conservation Association, and the Coalition of National Park Service Retirees.[267] On March 20, the NRA filed a notice to appeal in Federal District Court in opposition to the preliminary injunction.

Senator Coburn also introduced a bill, the Protecting Americans from Violent Crime Act of 2008 (S. 2619), that was very similar to his proposed amendment and DOI's proposed regulations. Supporters of those proposals pointed to a reported rise in illegal activities and violent crime on public lands. Opponents argued that the risk of a violent crime encounter in National Parks and Wildlife Refuges was negligible.[268] They further argued that allowing others to carry loaded and concealed handguns on their person would make them less safe. In the 111th Congress, similar measures were introduced by Representative Doc Hastings and Senator Mike Crapo (H.R. 1684/S. 816).

---

[261] 36 C.F.R. Part 2.

[262] 50 C.F.R. Part 27.

[263] Warren Richey, "Bid to Allow Guns in National Parks," *Christian Science Monitor*, August 19, 2008, p. 3.

[264] 73 *Federal Register* 23388.

[265] 73 *Federal Register* 39272.

[266] Department of the Interior, National Park Service, "General Regulations for Areas Administered by the National Park Service and the Fish and Wildlife Service," 73 *Federal Register* 74966-74972, December 10, 2008.

[267] Juliet Eilperin and Del Quentin Wilber, "Judge Blocks Rule Permitting Concealed Guns in U.S. Parks," *Washington Post*, March 20, 2009, p. A09.

[268] CRS compilation of *FBI Uniform Crime Reports* data show that from 2002 through 2006, there were 15 murders and non-negligent homicides reported by the FWS and 48 reported by the NPS. However, FWS reports all crimes encountered by its agents, whether or not they occurred on refuge land. It is difficult to determine how many of the 15 murders occurred on refuges.

Amtrak Passengers and Firearms

On September 16, 2010, Senator Roger Wicker amended the FY2010 Transportation-HUD appropriations bill (H.R. 3288) with language to authorize private persons to carry firearms and ammunition in their checked luggage on Amtrak trains. The Wicker amendment (S.Amdt. 2366) passed by a yea-nay vote, 68-30 (Record Vote Number 279). On September 17, 2009, the Senate passed this bill. Later, H.R. 3288 became the vehicle for the Consolidated Appropriations Act, 2010. Conferees retained the Wicker language in the conference agreement (H.Rept. 111-366), and the President signed H.R. 3288 into law (P.L. 111-117) on December 16, 2009. Section 159 of the act requires Amtrak, with the Transportation Security Administration, to report to Congress (within six months of enactment—June 16, 2010) on proposed guidance and procedures to implement a "checked firearms program." The reported guidance and procedures are to be implemented within one year of enactment. The act further requires that checked firearms be placed in a locked, hard-sided container, and that passengers planning to carry firearms in their luggage declare their intentions to Amtrak at the time they make their reservations or within 24 hours of departure. Similar requirements are set out for placing ammunition in checked luggage.

Law Enforcement Officers Safety Act Amendments

The 111th Congress passed amendments to clarify and expand eligibility under the Law Enforcement Officers Safety Act (LEOSA; P.L. 108-277). This law authorizes certain qualified active-duty and retired law enforcement officers to carry concealed firearms across state lines, while off duty. Senator Leahy, the Judiciary Committee chair, introduced the amendments as a stand-alone bill (S. 1132). In the House, Representative J. Randy Forbes introduced a similar measure (H.R. 3752). The Senate Judiciary Committee approved S. 1132 on March 11, 2010, and the Senate passed the bill on May 13, 2010. The Senate Judiciary Committee filed a report on this bill on July 27, 2010 (S.Rept. 111-233). The House passed S. 1132 on September 29, 2010. The President signed S. 1132 into law on October 12, 2010 (P.L. 111-272). The 2010 LEOSA amendments (1) clarify that certain Amtrak and executive branch law enforcement officers are eligible for concealed carry privileges under P.L. 108-277, (2) reduce the length of service criterion for eligibility under that law from 15 to 10 years, and (3) clarify other provisions of the law related to certification and credentialing.

Previously, in the 110th Congress, the Senate Judiciary Committee reported a similar bill (S. 376; S.Rept. 110-150) on September 5, 2007. This bill was also introduced by Senator Leahy. Representative Forbes introduced a similar bill (H.R. 2726). The language of S. 376 was incorporated into S. 2084, the School Safety and Law Enforcement Improvement Act of 2007, when that bill was reported on September 21, 2007 (S.Rept. 110-183). In the 109th Congress, the Senate amended H.R. 1751, the Court Security Improvement Act of 2006, with similar LEOSA provisions and passed that measure.

Patient Protection and Affordable Care Act and Firearms

The 111th Congress included language in the Patient Protection and Affordable Care Act (PPACA; P.L. 111-148) that prohibits data collection on gun ownership or higher premiums for gun owners under wellness program provisions. The catalyst for this language was an "action alert" that Gun Owners of America (GOA) sent out, urging its membership to oppose a Senate health care reform proposal released on November 18, 2009. The GOA argued that the Senate proposal, along with other enacted provisions of law, would have required doctors to provide "gun-related health data" to a computerized national health information network.[269] With such information, the GOA maintained that the federal government would deny individuals the ability to obtain a firearm or firearms permit. Of particular concern for the GOA were mental health records. Another concern raised by the GOA was the possibility that insurance providers under the Senate proposal would have been required or prompted to raise premiums for persons who exhibited arguably "unhealthy behaviors," such as firearms ownership.

Although the Senate proposal included provisions to amend the Health Insurance Portability and Accountability Act (HIPAA) that addressed electronic data transaction standards for national health information sharing purposes to facilitate eligibility determinations and health care plan enrollments, it did not include any provisions that would have directly required the national collection of "gun-related health data." Without a clear directive, it is debatable whether the Department of Health and Human Services (HHS) would have undertaken such data collection on firearms ownership and possession given other provisions in current law, albeit in different statutory contexts, that prohibit the establishment of a registry of privately held firearms or firearms owners.[270] Dr. David Blumenthal, the National Coordinator for Health Information Technology at HHS, said that the current system does not include a database into which such information could be fed, nor are there plans to create one.[271] Blumenthal added that "we don't want to do it and it's not authorized."[272]

Nor did the Senate proposal include any provisions that would have required or prompted insurance providers to raise premiums on gun owners. On the other hand, the Senate legislation did include provisions that would have codified and amended HIPAA wellness program provisions that would have addressed employer-based incentives for healthy behavior to reduce health care costs. Arguably, these provisions would not have precluded the Secretary of Health and Human Services from promulgating regulations that addressed risks associated with firearms ownership, possession, use, and storage. However, such regulations, if proposed, would have likely been tested in administrative and judicial review as to their impact on Second Amendment rights. Nonetheless, Senate legislators included new language in their Patient Protection and Affordable Care proposal, which the Senate passed as an amendment to H.R. 3590 on December 24, 2009.[273]

The Senate language, which was included in P.L. 111-148, prohibits any wellness and health promotion activity sponsored under the act's HIPAA amendments from requiring the disclosure or collection of any information about the presence or storage of a lawfully possessed firearm or ammunition in the residence or on the property of an individual, or the lawful use, possession, or storage of a firearm or ammunition by an individual. The language also states that nothing in the bill would be construed to authorize any data collection on the lawful ownership, possession, use, or storage of firearms or ammunition, or to maintain records on individual ownership or

---

[269] Shalaigh Murray, "Public Option at Center of Debate; Democratic Dissent Reid Must Find Compromise to Pass Health-Care Bill," *Washington Post*, November 23, 2009, p. A01.

[270] In the Brady Handgun Violence Prevention Act (P.L. 103-159, November 30, 1993, 107 Stat. 1542), Congress included a provision (§103(i)) that prohibits any department, agency, officer, or employee of the United States from establishing a registration system with respect to firearms, firearms owners, or firearms transactions/dispositions that would use records generated by the National Instant Criminal Background Check System (NICS).

[271] Peter Overby, "A Vote For Health Care, A Vote Against Gun Rights?," *National Public Radio*, November 25, 2009.

[272] Ibid.

[273] See proposed §2717 as included in §1001 and amended by §10101 in the Senate-passed H.R. 3590.

---

possession of a firearm or ammunition. In addition, with regard to any health insurance to be provided under the act, this provision prohibits providers from increasing premium rates; denying coverage; or reducing or withholding discounts, rebates, or rewards for participation in a wellness program because of an individual's lawful ownership, possession, use, or storage of a firearm or ammunition. Finally, under the data collection activities authorized under the act, the language states that no individual would be required to disclose any information relating to the lawful ownership, possession, use, or storage of a firearm or ammunition.

NICS Improvement Amendments Act of 2007[274]

In the wake of the Virginia Tech tragedy,[275] the 110th Congress passed legislation to improve firearms-related background checks. The Senate amended and passed the NICS Improvement Amendments Act of 2007 (H.R. 2640) following lengthy negotiations, as did the House, on December 19, 2007, clearing that bill for the President's signature. President Bush signed the bill into law on January 8, 2008 (P.L. 110-180). This law amends and strengthens a provision of the Brady Handgun Violence Prevention Act (Brady Act; P.L. 103-159) that requires federal agencies to provide, and the Attorney General to secure, any government records with information relevant to determining the eligibility of a person to receive a firearm for inclusion in databases queried by NICS.

The act also includes provisions designed to encourage states, tribes, and territories (states) to make available to the Attorney General certain records related to persons who are disqualified from acquiring a firearm, particularly records related to domestic violence misdemeanor convictions and restraining orders, as well as mental health adjudications. To accomplish this, the act establishes a framework of incentives and disincentives, whereby the Attorney General is authorized to either waive a grant match requirement or reduce a law enforcement assistance grant depending upon a state's compliance with the act's goals of bringing firearms-related disqualifying records online.

The original proposal (H.R. 2640) was introduced by Representative McCarthy and co-sponsored by Representative John Dingell. As passed by the House by a voice vote on June 13, 2007, H.R. 2640 reportedly reflected a compromise between groups favoring and opposing greater gun control.[276] The Senate Judiciary Committee approved similar, but not identical, NICS improvement amendments as part of the School Safety and Law Enforcement Improvement Act of 2004 on August 2, 2007, and reported this bill on September 21, 2007 (S. 2084; S.Rept. 110-183). The Senate Judiciary Committee included five other measures in S. 2084. With some modification, those measures included the School Safety Improvements Act (S. 1217), the Equity in Law Enforcement Act (S. 1448), the PRECAUTION Act (S. 1521), the Terrorist Hoax Improvements Act (S. 735), and the Law Enforcement Officers Safety Act of 2007 (LEOSA; S. 376). Support for the NICS improvement and the LEOSA amendments (described below) in S.

---

[274] As described in greater detail above, the National Instant Criminal Background Check System (NICS) is administered by the FBI, so that federally licensed gun dealers can process a background check to determine a customer's eligibility to possess a firearm before proceeding with a transaction.

[275] On April 16, 2007, a student at Virginia Polytechnic Institute and State University shot 32 people to death and wounded many others.

[276] Jonathan Weisman, "Democrats, NRA Reach Deal on Background-Check Bill," *Washington Post*, June 10, 2007, p. A02.

2084 was reportedly divided and uneven, however.[277] Citing privacy and cost issues related to the NICS amendments, Senator Coburn reportedly placed a hold on that legislation.[278]

In addition, some opposition to NICS improvement amendments had coalesced around an assertion made by Larry Pratt of Gun Owners of America that, under these amendments, any veteran who was or had been diagnosed with Posttraumatic Stress Disorder (PTSD)[279] and was found to be a "danger to himself or others would have his gun rights taken away ... forever."[280] Under current law, however, any veteran or other VA beneficiary who is adjudicated or determined to be a mental defective, because he poses a danger to himself or others, or is incapable of conducting his day-to-day affairs, is ineligible to possess a firearm. A diagnosis of PTSD in and of itself is not a disqualifying factor for the purposes of gun control under the NICS improvement amendments or previous law. Under the enacted NICS improvement amendments, VA beneficiaries who have been determined to be mental defectives could appeal for administrative relief and possibly have their gun rights restored if they could demonstrate that they were no longer afflicted by a disqualifying condition.

Veterans, Mental Incompetency, and Firearms Eligibility

In the 110th Congress, Senator Burr successfully amended the Veterans' Medical Personnel Recruitment and Retention Act of 2008 (S. 2969) in full committee markup on June 26, 2008. The language of the Burr amendment would have provided that "a veteran, surviving spouse, or child who is mentally incapacitated, deemed mentally incompetent, or experiencing an extended loss of consciousness shall not be considered adjudicated as a mental defective" for purposes of the Gun Control Act, "without the order or finding of a judge, magistrate, or other judicial authority of competent jurisdiction that such veteran, surviving spouse, or child is a danger to him or herself or others." Senator Burr introduced a bill, the Veterans' 2nd Amendment Protection Act (S. 3167), that would have achieved the same ends as his amendment to S. 2969.

In the 111th Congress, Senator Burr reintroduced his bill as S. 669, and the Senate Committee on Veterans' Affairs reported this bill (S.Rept. 111-27) on June 16, 2009. Representative Jerry Moran introduced a similar bill (H.R. 2547). The House Veterans' Affairs Committee considered and approved a similar provision that Representative John Boozman offered as an amendment to a draft bill in full committee markup on September 15, 2010. This provision was included in the reported version of the bill (H.R. 6132; H.Rept. 111-630). However, when the House considered H.R. 6132 under suspension of the rules, an amended version of H.R. 6132 was called up that did not include the Boozman provision.

---

[277] David Rogers, "Democrats Stall on Gun-Records Bill: Despite Support, Background-Check Measure Staggers in Senate Amid Infighting," *Wall Street Journal*, September 21, 2007, p. A6.

[278] Seth Stern, "Coburn Blocks Gun Background-Check Bill, Citing Concerns About Privacy, Spending," *CQ Today*, September 25, 2007.

[279] PTSD is an anxiety disorder that can occur after one has been through a traumatic event. Symptoms may manifest soon after the trauma, or may be delayed. For further information, see U.S. Department of Veterans Affairs, National Center for Posttraumatic Stress Disorder, Fact Sheet, http://www.ncptsd.va.gov/ncmain/ncdocs/fact_shts/ fs_what_is_ptsd html.

[280] Larry Pratt, "Veterans Disarmament Act To Bar Vets From Owning Guns," September 23, 2007, http://www.prisonplanet.com/articles/september2007/230907Disarmament.htm.

Mental Defective Adjudications

Under 27 C.F.R. Section 478.11, the term "adjudicated as a mental defective" includes a determination by a court, board, commission, or other lawful authority that a person, as a result of marked subnormal intelligence or a mental illness, incompetency, condition, or disease, (1) is a danger to himself or others, or (2) lacks the mental capacity to manage his own affairs. The term also includes (1) a finding of insanity by a court in a criminal case and (2) those persons found incompetent to stand trial or found not guilty by reason of lack of mental responsibility pursuant to articles 50a and 72b of the Uniform Code of Military Justice, 10 U.S.C. Sections 850a, 876(b).

This definition of "mental defective" was promulgated by the ATF in a final rule published on June 27, 1997.[281] In the final rule, the ATF noted that the VA had commented on the "proposed rulemaking" and had correctly interpreted that "adjudicated as a mental defective" includes a person who is found to be "mentally incompetent" by the Veterans Benefit Administration (VBA). Under veterans law, an individual is considered "mentally incompetent" if he or she lacks the mental capacity to contract or manage his or her own affairs for reasons related to injury or disease (under 38 CFR §3.353).[282] In a proposed rulemaking, the ATF opined that the inclusion of "mentally incompetent" in the definition of "mental defective" was wholly consistent with the legislative history of the 1968 Gun Control Act.[283] Reportedly, the VA could have been the only federal agency that had promulgated a definition like "mentally incompetent" that overlapped with the term "mental defective."[284]

VA Referrals to the FBI

In November 1998, the VBA provided the FBI with disqualifying records on 88,898 VA beneficiaries. VA rating specialists had determined based upon medical evidence that these beneficiaries were unable to manage their own financial affairs.[285] The VA appointed a fiduciary for purposes of receiving and managing each beneficiary's VA benefits. According to the VA, during the determination process beneficiaries were notified that VA proposed to rate them "incompetent" and that they were able to request a hearing and submit evidence to the contrary if they wished. VA also advised these beneficiaries regarding their right to appeal any final rating regarding their ability to receive and manage their own VA benefits. Despite the resultant NICS referral, however, the VA did not necessarily inform the beneficiary that he would lose his gun rights as a consequence of this determination. As described above, under the P.L. 110-180 the VA is required to inform the beneficiary of this outcome.

Interestingly, the Veterans Medical Administration has not submitted any disqualifying records on VA medical care recipients to the FBI for inclusion in NICS for any medical/psychiatric reason (like PTSD). While veterans with PTSD or any other condition, who have been involuntarily committed under a state court order to a VA medical facility because they posed a danger to themselves or others, are ineligible to ship, transport, receive, or possess a firearm or ammunition

---

[281] *Federal Register*, vol. 62, no. 124, June 27, 1997, p. 34634.

[282] *Federal Register*, vol. 61, no. 174, September 6, 1996, p. 47095.

[283] Ibid.

[284] Personal communication with Compensation and Pension Program staff, Department of Veterans Affairs, July 9, 2008.

[285] Personal communication with the Office of Congressional Affairs staff, Department of Veterans Affairs, February 10, 2012.

under federal law, the Veterans Medical Administration would not make a related referral about that ineligibility to the FBI. Instead, the state in which the court resides would submit the disqualifying record to the FBI, if such a submission would be appropriate and permissible under state law.[286]

Nevertheless, the decision by the VA to submit VBA records on "mentally incompetent" veterans to the FBI for inclusion in the NICS mental defective file generated some degree of controversy in 1999 and 2000.[287] Critics of this policy underscored that veterans routinely consented to "mentally incompetent" determinations so that a fiduciary (designated payee) could be appointed for them. Those critics contended that to take away a veteran's Second Amendment rights without his foreknowledge was improper. They also pointed out that no other federal agencies were providing similar disqualifying records to the FBI. This controversy subsided, but it re-emerged when Congress considered the NICS improvement amendments (described above).

According to the Bureau of Justice Statistics, as of May 1, 2011, there were 130,886 files in the NICS mental defective file, which had been referred to the FBI by the VA. Those VA files accounted for 99.2% of mental defective files (131,979) referred to the FBI by any federal department or agency. In the view of some Members of Congress, it may be incongruous that other federal agencies, such as the Social Security Administration, that provide similar disability and income maintenance benefits to persons who are mentally incapacitated refer relatively few, if any, firearms-related disqualifying records about beneficiaries whom they serve to the FBI. Moreover, there are other individuals in the U.S. population who are similarly incapacitated due to their age-related infirmities or mental disabilities, but in many cases there are no mechanisms for state or local authorities to make similar referrals to the FBI. As a consequence, even with the changes put in place by P.L. 110-180, those Members of Congress may view the VA's continued referral of firearms-related disqualifying records on veterans who have had a fiduciary appointed on their behalf but have not behaved in a threatening or dangerous manner to be an unjustified indignity placed on individuals who have served their country honorably in the Armed Forces.

Other Members of Congress would maintain that the VA has faithfully complied with the law and that public safety is enhanced by making those referrals to the FBI. They might also argue that opposition to the VA policy waned between November 1998 and the 2007 congressional debate, demonstrating that veterans who were "adjudicated mental defective," rarely, if ever, sought to acquire and were subsequently denied firearms in a manner that could be described as an injustice. Those Members would likely underscore that, in their view, the VA's current policy does not diminish national recognition of those veterans' honorable service. Rather, the VA's policy has been implemented to protect those veterans and others from the harm that might result if they acquired a firearm and used it improperly due to reasons possibly related to their mental incompetency.

---

[286] For further information on the treatment of mental illness and substance abuse for the purposes of gun control, see Donna M. Norris, M.D., et al., "Firearm Laws, Patients, and the Roles of Psychiatrists," *American Journal of Psychiatry*, August 2006, pp. 1392-1396.

[287] John Dougherty, "VA Give FBI Health Secrets: Veterans' Records Could Block Firearms Purchases," *WorldNet Daily.com*, June 22, 2000; and "VA Defends Vets' Records Transfers to NICS System," *New Gun Week*, vol. 35, issue 1650, July 10, 2000, p. 1.

Public Housing and Firearms Possession and Use

In the 110th Congress, the House passed a bill (H.R. 6216) on July 9, 2008, that would have made changes related to the administration of the public housing program administered by the Department of Housing and Urban Development (HUD) through local public housing authorities (PHAs). The bill includes a provision that would have prohibited the HUD Secretary from accepting as reasonable any management or related fees charged by a PHA for enforcing any provision of a lease agreement that requires tenants to register firearms that are otherwise legally possessed, or that prohibits their possession outright. On the other hand, the bill would have allowed PHAs to terminate the lease of any tenant who was found to be illegally using a firearm.

The gun-related provision in H.R. 6216 reportedly reflected a compromise.[288] The original language restricting fees for enforcing gun restrictions was included in a motion to recommit offered during floor debate on a similar public housing bill (H.R. 3521). That bill was not approved by the House, but was sent back to the House Financial Services Committee for further consideration. A new version of the public housing bill (H.R. 5829) was introduced that included language from the motion to recommit, but it did not include the lease termination proviso, and the bill received no further consideration.

In the 111th Congress, the Financial Services Committee reported the Section 8 Voucher Reform Act of 2009 (H.R. 3045; H.Rept. 111-277) on July 23, 2009. In committee markup, Representative Price successfully amended the bill on July 9, 2009, with language that would have prevented authorities from prohibiting firearms in public housing. The committee approved another housing bill that included a similar provision (H.R. 4868) on July 27, 2010.

Concealed Carry and Reciprocity (Thune Amendment)

On July 22, 2009, the Senate considered an amendment (S.Amdt. 1618) offered by Senator Thune to the FY2010 Defense Authorization Act (S. 1390) that would have arguably provided for national reciprocity between states regarding the concealed carry of firearms. By agreement, the amendment needed 60 votes to pass, but it was narrowly defeated by a recorded vote, 58-39. Senator Thune introduced a similar bill, the Respecting States Rights and Concealed Carry Reciprocity Act of 2009 (S. 845).

As background, the issue of concealed carry under state law can be divided into four categories: (1) no permit required, (2) mandatory or "shall issue," (3) discretionary or "may issue," and (4) no concealed carry permitted. In Alaska and Vermont, state law allowed concealed carry without a permit (no permit required), as is the case today. When the Thune amendment was debated, 35 states had "shall issue" laws, in that the state issues the permit as long as the applicant meets the eligibility criteria.[289] Eleven states were "may issue" states, in that the state had discretion in

---

[288] Seth Stern, "House to Try Again on Public Housing Bill," *CQ Today*, July 8, 2008.

[289] At the time of the Thune amendment, "shall issue" states included Alaska, Arizona, Arkansas, Colorado, Florida, Georgia, Idaho, Indiana, Kansas, Kentucky, Louisiana, Maine, Michigan, Minnesota, Mississippi, Missouri, Montana, Nebraska, Nevada, New Hampshire, New Mexico, North Carolina, North Dakota, Ohio, Oklahoma, Oregon, Pennsylvania, South Carolina, South Dakota, Tennessee, Texas, Utah, Virginia, Washington, West Virginia, and Wyoming.

whether to issue a permit.[290] And, Wisconsin and Illinois state law prohibited the concealed carry of firearms by civilians under any circumstances.

Many states with concealed carry laws have extended concealed carry privileges, or reciprocity, to the residents of other states. According to the NRA, however, those concealed carry laws are often very technical and subject to change. Moreover, there are no national eligibility criteria, or training standards regarding concealed carry. Although the Thune amendment did not address the issue of national standards, it arguably would have required "may issue" states to honor the permits issued by "shall issue" states. By extension, it would also have required "shall issue" and "may issue" states to honor the eligibility of all residents of Alaska and Vermont to carry concealed firearms in their states, as long as those persons were not otherwise prohibited from possessing firearms.

Bankruptcy and Firearms

Representative John A. Boccieri and Senator Leahy introduced the Protecting Gun Owners in Bankruptcy Act of 2010 (H.R. 5827/S. 3654). This proposal would have amended federal bankruptcy law to permit an individual to exempt from the property of his estate a single rifle, shotgun, or pistol, or any combination thereof, as long as the total value of the exemption did not exceed $3,000. On July 28, 2010, the House passed H.R. 5827 by a roll call vote (two-thirds required) of 307-113 (Roll no. 479). In the 112th Congress, Representative Tim Griffin has introduced a similar measure (H.R. 1181).

ATF Appropriations and Southwest Border Gun Trafficking

The 111th Congress considered legislation to either fund ATF or authorize increased appropriations for the agency. The ATF enforces federal criminal law related to the manufacture, importation, and distribution of alcohol, tobacco, firearms, and explosives. ATF works both independently and through partnerships with industry groups; international, state, and local governments; and other federal agencies to investigate and reduce crime involving firearms and explosives, acts of arson, and illegal trafficking of alcohol and tobacco products.

ATF Appropriations for FY2011[291]

The President's FY2011 budget request included $1.163 billion for ATF, an increase of $42.2 million, or 3.8%, compared to the FY2010-enacted appropriation. Proposed increases (over base) included $11.8 million for Project Gunrunner[292] and $1.2 million for Emergency Support Function #13 (ESF-13), the Public Safety and Security Annex to the National Response Framework (NRF).[293] The NRF sets broad responsibilities and lines of authority for federal

---

[290] "May issue" states included Alabama, Connecticut, and Iowa. The following states are restrictive may issue states: California, Delaware, Hawaii, Maryland, Massachusetts, New Jersey, New York, and Rhode Island.

[291] For further information, see CRS Report R41206, *The Bureau of Alcohol, Tobacco, Firearms and Explosives (ATF): Budget and Operations for FY2011*, by William J. Krouse.

[292] For further information on Operation Gunrunner, see CRS Report R40733, *Gun Trafficking and the Southwest Border*, by Vivian S. Chu and William J. Krouse.

[293] For more information, see CRS Report RL34758, *The National Response Framework: Overview and Possible Issues for Congress*, by Bruce R. Lindsay.

agencies in the event of a national emergency or major disaster. Under the NRF, the Attorney General is responsible for ESF-13, which entails all hazards law enforcement planning and coordination for the entire United States and its territories. The Attorney General, in turn, has delegated his responsibility for ESF-13's implementation to the ATF. On July 22, 2010, the Senate Appropriations Committee reported an FY2011 CJS appropriations bill (S. 3636; S.Rept. 111-229). This measure would have provided ATF with $1.163 billion for FY2011, matching the Administration's request. On July 22, 2010, the Senate Appropriations Committee marked up and reported the FY2011 Commerce, Justice, Science, and Related Agencies (CJS) appropriations bill (S. 3636). The Senate bill would have matched the Administration's request. In the absence of an enacted CJS appropriations bill, Congress passed several continuing resolutions.[294] As described above, the 112th Congress finalized the FY2011 ATF appropriation and provided the agency with $1.113 billion.

ATF Appropriations for FY2010[295]

For FY2010, the Administration requested $1.121 billion and 5,025 full-time equivalent (FTE) positions for ATF, or $66.6 million and 68 FTE positions more than the amounts appropriated for FY2009 ($1.054 billion and 4,957). Of the difference, $23.6 million and 22 FTE positions were base adjustments. For Southwest border enforcement, the FY2010 request included a budget enhancement of $18 million to support Project Gunrunner and $25 million for the new National Center for Explosives Training and Research Center (NCETR). Compared to the enacted FY2009 level of funding, the FY2010 request would have provided a 4.9% increase.

For ATF, Congress appropriated $1.121 billion in the Consolidated Appropriations Act, 2010 (H.R. 3288). The President signed this bill into law on December 16, 2009 (P.L. 111-117).[296] The act provided an amount that was equal to the Administration's request. This amount was $52.5 million more than the final FY2009-enacted amount, or an increase of 4.9%. Conference report language (H.Rept. 111-366) indicated that the act included $18 million for Project Gunrunner, the same amount requested by the Administration. In addition, the act also included $10 million to increase the Violent Crime Impact Team program, $6 million for construction (phase two) of the NCETR, and $1.5 million to complete ATF headquarters construction projects.

On July 28, 2010, the House passed an FY2010 supplemental appropriations bill (H.R. 5875) that included $39.1 million for ATF to increase Southwest border gun trafficking investigations. On August 5, 2010, the Senate passed its version of H.R. 5875, which included $37.5 million for ATF. On August 9, the House introduced a new border security supplemental bill (H.R. 6080), which was subsequently passed by the House on August 10. This bill contained language identical to Senate-passed H.R. 5875. Reportedly, the House took up the bill with a new number to avoid a dispute related to its constitutional obligation to originate all revenue measures.[297] This

---

[294] For further information, see CRS Report RL30343, *Continuing Resolutions: Latest Action and Brief Overview of Recent Practices*, by Sandy Streeter.

[295] For further information, see CRS Report RL34514, *The Bureau of Alcohol, Tobacco, Firearms and Explosives (ATF): Budget and Operations for FY2008, FY2009, and FY2010*, by William J. Krouse.

[296] The conference report on the bill includes provisions for six of the seven FY2010 appropriations: Transportation-HUD; Commerce-Justice-Science; Financial Services; Labor-HHS; Military Construction-VA; and State-Foreign Operations. The Defense appropriations bill, H.R. 3326, was passed separately.

[297] Theo Emery and Edward Epstein, "Border Security Bill Passes in House," *CQ Today*, August 10, 2010, online edition.

---

dispute arose with the addition of funding provisions in Senate-passed H.R. 5875 that were not included in the House-passed version. On August 12, the Senate passed H.R. 6080. On August 13, the President signed H.R. 6080 into law (P.L. 111-230). It provides ATF with an additional $37.5 million for Project Gunrunner.

Southwest Border Gun Trafficking

On the Southwest border with Mexico, firearms violence has spiked sharply in recent years as drug trafficking organizations have reportedly vied for control of key smuggling corridors into the United States. In March 2008, President Felipe Calderón called on the United States to increase its efforts to suppress gun trafficking from the United States into Mexico. In the 110th Congress, the House passed a bill (H.R. 6028) that would authorize a total of $73.5 million to be appropriated over three years, for FY2008 through FY2010, to increase ATF resources dedicated to stemming illegal gun trafficking into Mexico as part of the Mérida Initiative.[298] Similar authorizations were included in S. 2867, H.R. 5863, and H.R. 5869. In the 111th Congress, similar authorizations were included in several bills (S. 205, H.R. 495, H.R. 1448, and H.R. 1867).

Tiahrt Amendment and Firearms Trace Data Limitations

Representative Todd Tiahrt offered an amendment that placed several funding restrictions and conditions on ATF and the FBI during full committee markup of the FY2004 DOJ appropriations bill (H.R. 2799). While modified, those restrictions were included in the Consolidated Appropriations Act, 2004 (P.L. 108-199). Amended to the ATF appropriations every year since (FY2005-FY2012), the Tiahrt restrictions

- prohibit the use of any funding appropriated for ATF to disclose firearms trace or multiple handgun sales report data for any purpose other than supporting "bona fide" criminal investigation or agency licensing proceedings,

- prohibit the use of any funding appropriated for ATF to issue new regulations that would require licensed dealers to conduct physical inventories of their businesses,

- require the next-day destruction of approved Brady background check records, and

- require ATF to include certain data disclaimers with any firearms tracing study it releases.

Of these limitations, the first, dealing with disclosure of firearms trace or multiple handgun sales report data, probably was and is the most contentious. A coalition of U.S. mayors, including New York City Mayor Michael Bloomberg, maintain that they should have access to such data in order to identify out-of-state federally licensed gun dealers who wittingly or unwittingly sell large numbers of firearms to illegal gun traffickers.

For FY2008, the Tiahrt limitation on firearms trace and multiple handgun sales report data was the source of debate when the Senate CJS Appropriations Subcommittee did not include this

---

[298] For further information, see CRS Report RS22837, *Mérida Initiative: U.S. Anticrime and Counterdrug Assistance for Mexico and Central America*, by Clare Ribando Seelke.

limitation in its draft bill. Senator Richard Shelby amended the FY2008 CJS appropriations bill (which became S. 1745) with similar, but modified, limitations in full committee markup. Similar language was included in the House-passed CJS appropriations bill (H.R. 3093), and was included in the Consolidated Appropriations Act, 2008 (P.L. 110-161; H.R. 2764), into which the CJS appropriations were folded.[299] The modified FY2008 limitation included new language that authorizes ATF to

- share firearms trace data with tribal and foreign law enforcement agencies and federal agencies for national intelligence purposes;

- share firearms trace data with law enforcement agencies and prosecutors to exchange among themselves; and

- release aggregate statistics on firearms traffickers and trafficking channels, or firearms misuse, felons, and trafficking investigations.

The FY2008 limitation, however, continued to prohibit the release of firearms trace data for the purposes of suing gun manufacturers and dealers. Moreover, the limitation includes the phrase "in fiscal year 2008 and thereafter," which made it permanent law according to the Government Accountability Office (GAO).[300] Despite the futurity language, Congress has modified the limitation's language and included it (with futurity language) in the FY2009, FY2010, FY2011, and FY2012 Commerce, Justice, Science (CJS), and Related Agencies Appropriations Acts (P.L. 111-8, P.L. 111-117, P.L. 112-10, and P.L. 112-55).

---

[299] For further information, see CRS Report RS22458, *Gun Control: Statutory Disclosure Limitations on ATF Firearms Trace Data and Multiple Handgun Sales Reports*, by William J. Krouse.

[300] U.S. Government Accountability Office, "Bureau of Alcohol, Tobacco, Firearms, and Explosives—Prohibition in the 2008 Consolidated Appropriations Act," July 15, 2008, http://www.gao.gov/decisions/appro/316510.pdf.

Appendix B. Major Federal Firearms and Related Statutes

The following principal changes to the Gun Control Act have been enacted since 1968.

- The Firearms Owners' Protection Act, McClure-Volkmer Amendments (P.L. 99-308, 1986), eases certain interstate transfer and shipment requirements for long guns, defines the term "engaged in the business," eliminates some recordkeeping requirements, and bans the private possession of machine guns not legally owned prior to 1986.

- The Armor Piercing Ammunition Ban (P.L. 99-408, 1986, amended in P.L. 103-322, 1994) prohibits the manufacture, importation, and delivery of handgun ammunition composed of certain metal substances and certain full-jacketed ammunition.

- The Federal Energy Management Improvement Act of 1988 (P.L. 100-615) requires that all toys or firearm look-a-likes have a blazed orange plug in the barrel, denoting that it is a non-lethal imitation.

- The Undetectable Firearms Act (P.L. 100-649, 1988, amended by P.L. 108-174, 2003), also known as the "plastic gun" legislation, bans the manufacture, import, possession, and transfer of firearms not detectable by security devices.

- The Gun-Free School Zone Act of 1990 (P.L. 101-647), as originally enacted, was ruled unconstitutional by the U.S. Supreme Court (*United States* v. *Lopez*, 514 U.S. 549 (1995), April 26, 1995). The act prohibited possession of a firearm in a school zone (on the campus of a public or private school or within 1,000 feet of the grounds). In response to the Court's finding that the act exceeded Congress's authority to regulate commerce, the 104th Congress included a provision in P.L. 104-208 that amended the act to require federal prosecutors to include evidence that the firearms "moved in" or affected interstate commerce.

- The Brady Handgun Violence Prevention Act, 1993 (P.L. 103-159), requires that background checks be completed on all non-licensed persons seeking to obtain firearms from federal firearms licensees.

- The Violent Crime Control and Law Enforcement Act of 1994 (P.L. 103-322) prohibited the manufacture or importation of semiautomatic assault weapons and large-capacity ammunition feeding devices for 10 years. The act also bans the sale or transfer of handguns and handgun ammunition to, or possession of handguns and handgun ammunition by, juveniles (younger than 18 years old) without prior written consent from the juvenile's parent or legal guardian; exceptions related to employment, ranching, farming, target practice, and hunting are provided. In addition, the act disqualifies persons under court orders related to domestic abuse from receiving a firearm from any person or possessing a firearm. It also increased penalties for the criminal use of firearms. The assault weapons ban expired on September 13, 2004.

- The Federal Domestic Violence Gun Ban (the Lautenberg Amendment, in the Omnibus Consolidated Appropriations Act for FY1997, P.L. 104-208) prohibits persons convicted of misdemeanor crimes of domestic violence from possessing firearms and ammunition. The ban applies regardless of when the offense was adjudicated: prior to, or following enactment. It has been challenged in the federal courts, but these challenges have been defeated.[301]

- The Omnibus Consolidated and Emergency Appropriations Act, 1999 (P.L. 105-277), requires all federal firearms licensees to offer for sale gun storage and safety devices. It also bans firearms transfers to, or possession by, most non-immigrants and those non-immigrants who have overstayed the terms of their temporary visa.

- The Treasury, Postal and General Government Appropriations Act (P.L. 106-58) requires that background checks be conducted when former firearms owners seek to reacquire a firearm that they sold to a pawnshop.

- The Homeland Security Act of 2002 (P.L. 107-296) establishes a Bureau of Alcohol, Tobacco, Firearms and Explosives by transferring the law enforcement functions, but not the revenue functions, of the former Bureau of Alcohol, Tobacco and Firearms from the Department of the Treasury to the Department of Justice.

- The Law Enforcement Officers Safety Act of 2004 (P.L. 108-277) provides that qualified active and retired law enforcement officers may carry a concealed firearm. This act supersedes state level prohibitions on concealed carry that would otherwise apply to law enforcement officers, but it does not override any federal laws. Nor does the act supersede or limit state laws that permit private persons or entities to prohibit or restrict the possession of concealed firearms on their property or prohibit or restrict the possession of firearms on any state or local government property, installation, building, base, or park.

- The Protection of Lawful Commerce in Arms Act (P.L. 109-92) prohibits certain types of lawsuits against firearms manufacturers and dealers to recover damages related to the criminal or unlawful use of their products (firearms and ammunition) by other persons.[302] This law also includes provisions that (1) increase penalties for using armor-piercing handgun ammunition in the commission of a crime of violence or drug trafficking, (2) require the Attorney General to submit a report (within two years of enactment) on "armor-piercing" ammunition based on certain performance characteristics, including barrel length and amount of propellant (gun powder), and (3) prohibits federally licensed gun dealers from transferring a handgun to an unlicensed person without also providing a secure storage or safety device.

- The Violence Against Women and Department of Justice Reauthorization Act of 2005 (P.L. 109-162) authorized to be appropriated for ATF the following amounts: $924 million for FY2006, $961 million for FY2007, $999 million for FY2008, and $1.039 billion for FY2009.

---

[301] See CRS Report RL31143, *Firearms Prohibitions and Domestic Violence Convictions: The Lautenberg Amendment*, by T. J. Halstead.

[302] For further information, see CRS Report RS22074, *Limiting Tort Liability of Gun Manufacturers and Gun Sellers: Legal Analysis of P.L. 109-92 (2005)*, by Henry Cohen.

- The USA PATRIOT Improvement and Reauthorization Act of 2005 (P.L. 109-177) includes a provision that requires that the ATF Director be appointed by the President with the advice and consent of the Senate.

- The Disaster Recovery Personal Protection Act of 2006, which was included in the Department of Homeland Security Appropriations Act, 2007 (P.L. 109-295), amended the Robert T. Stafford Disaster Relief and Emergency Assistance Act (42 U.S.C. §5207) to prohibit federal officials from seizing or authorizing the seizure of any firearm from private persons during a major disaster or emergency if possession of that firearm was not already prohibited under federal or state law. It also forbids the same officials from prohibiting the possession of any firearm that is not otherwise prohibited. Also, the law bans any prohibition on carrying firearms by persons who are otherwise permitted to legally carry such firearms because those persons are working under a federal agency, or under the control of an agency, providing disaster or emergency relief.

Author Contact Information

William J. Krouse
Specialist in Domestic Security and Crime Policy
wkrouse@crs.loc.gov, 7-2225